1st Workshop on Linguistic Insights from and for Multimodal Language Processing (LIMO 2023)

Ingolstadt, Germany
22 September 2023

ISBN: 979-8-3313-1647-1

Printed from e-media with permission by:

Curran Associates, Inc.
57 Morehouse Lane
Red Hook, NY 12571

Some format issues inherent in the e-media version may also appear in this print version.

Association for Computational Linguistics
209 N. Eighth Street
Stroudsburg, Pennsylvania 18360

Phone: 1-570-476-8006
Fax: 1-570-476-0860

acl@aclweb.org

Additional copies of this publication are available from:

Curran Associates, Inc.
57 Morehouse Lane
Red Hook, NY 12571 USA
Phone: 845-758-0400
Fax: 845-758-2633
Email: curran@proceedings.com
Web: www.proceedings.com

LIMO 2023

The 1st Workshop on Linguistic Insights from and for Multimodal Language Processing

Proceedings of the Workshop

September 22, 2023

Order copies of this and other ACL proceedings from:

Association for Computational Linguistics (ACL)
209 N. Eighth Street
Stroudsburg, PA 18360
USA
Tel: +1-570-476-8006
Fax: +1-570-476-0860
acl@aclweb.org

Foreword

Processing multimodal information (like visual representations of the environment, auditory cues, images, gestures, gaze etc.) and integrating them is a constant and effortless process in human language processing. Recent progress in the area of language & vision, large-scale visually grounded language models, and multimodal learning (e. g. CLIP (Radford et al., 2021), VILBERT (Lu et al., 2019) etc.) have led to breakthroughs in challenging multimodal NLP applications like image-text retrieval, image captioning (Cornia et al., 2020) or visual question answering (Antol et al., 2015). Yet, modeling the semantics and pragmatics of situated language understanding and generation and, generally, language processing beyond the linguistic context, i. e. in combination with multiple other modalities, is still one of the biggest challenges in NLP and Computational Linguistics (Bisk et al., 2020).

Recent efforts in understanding complex multimodal phenomena in language and dialogue have explored a variety of aspects of multimodality and produced a substantial amount of valuable multimodal datasets and models that include various types of text (from short and informal social media comments to more formal news, instructions/manuals and legal documents, they are also usually accompanied by an image, meme, animation or video) and dialogue (from reference games, instruction dialogues to fully situated interaction with agents and robots). The variety in this wide problem space and the downstream tasks also require variety in the approaches to tackle them. As a result, Multimodal Language Processing is approached by many different sub-areas of Computational Linguistics and NLP—in computational semantics and pragmatics, dialogue modeling, language modeling, and grounding, multimodal and crossmodal learning, and beyond, including physical or robotic actions.

While there have been recent venues and workshops targeting multimodal representation learning and large-scale Language and Vision models, there is a lack of discussion in the community that focuses on linguistic multimodal phenomena, domain- and task-specific analyses of multimodality and, generally, contributions of computational linguistics to multimodal learning and vice versa (Parcalabescu et al., 2022). With this workshop, we aim to bring together researchers who work on various linguistic aspects of multimodal language processing to discuss and share the recent advances in this interdisciplinary field.

The main goals of this workshop are to

- Discuss various tasks, phenomena, models, and problems in multimodal language processing
- Discuss how insights from (computational) linguistics can inform multimodal learning and modeling
- Facilitate networking and encourage collaboration between researchers working on different aspects of multimodality in computational linguistics and language processing

The LIMO 2023 workshop organizers:
Piush Aggarwal, Özge Alaçam, Carina Silberer, Sina Zarrieß and Torsten Zesch

Organizing Committee

Piush Aggarwal (FernUniversität in Hagen)

Özge Alaçam (Universität Bielefeld)

Carina Silberer (Universität Stuttgart)

Sina Zarrieß (Universität Bielefeld)

Torsten Zesch (FernUniversität in Hagen)

Program Committee

Albert Gatt (Utrecht University, Netherlands)

Animesh Mukherjee (IIT-Kharagpur, India)

Asif Ekbal (IIT-Patna, India)

Barbara Plank (LMU Munich, Germany)

Corentin Kervadec (Universitat Pompeu Fabra, Spain)

David Schlangen (University of Potsdam, Germany)

Desmond Elliott (University of Copenhagen, Denmark)

Hsiu-Yu Yang (Institute for Computational Linguistics, Stuttgart University, Germany)

Jana Götze (University of Potsdam, Germany)

Letitia Parcalabescu (Heidelberg University, Germany)

Nikolai Ilinykh (University of Gothenburg, Sweden)

Sabine Schulte im Walde (Universität Stuttgart, Germany)

Sandro Pezzelle (ILLC, University of Amsterdam, Netherlands)

Seid Muhie Yimam (University of Hamburg, Germany)

Sherzod Hakimovn (University of Potsdam, Germany)

Simon Dobnik (University of Gothenburg, Sweden)

Timo Baumann (OTH Regensburg, Germany)

Invited Speakers

Letitia Parcalabescu (Heidelberg University, Germany)

Sandro Pezzelle (ILLC, University of Amsterdam, Netherlands)

Table of Contents

Conference Program

Friday, September 22, 2023

9:00–9:10 ***Kick-off for LIMO workshop***

9:10–9:30 **2 Min. Teaser for Accepted Papers**

A Pipeline for the Creation of Multimodal Corpora from YouTube Videos
Nathan Dykes, Anna Wilson and Peter Uhrig

Multi-Modal Learning Application – Support Language Learners with NLP Techniques and Eye-Tracking
Robert Geislinger, Ali Ebrahimi Pourasad, Deniz Gül, Daniel Djahangir, Seid Muhie Yimam, Steffen Remus and Chris Biemann

Context matters: evaluation of target and context features on variation of object naming
Nikolai Ilinykh and Simon Dobnik

The Scenario Refiner: Grounding subjects in images at the morphological level
Claudia C. Tagliaferri, Denis Paperno, Albert Gatt and Sofia Axioti

FlowchartQA: The First Large-Scale Benchmark for Reasoning over Flowcharts
Simon Tannert, Marcelo G. Feighelstein, Jasmina Bogojeska, Joseph Shtok, Assaf Arbelle, Peter W. J. Staar, Anika Schumann, Jonas Kuhn and Leonid Karlinsky

Presenting an Annotation Pipeline for Fine-grained Linguistic Analyses of Multimodal Corpora
Elena Volkanovska, Sherry Tan, Changxu Duan, Debajyoti Chowdhury and Sabine Bartsch

9:30–10:30 *Invited Talk by Dr. Letitia Parcalabescu*

10:30–10:50 ***Coffee Break***

Friday, September 22, 2023 (continued)

10:50–12:00 Poster Session

12:00–13:00 *Invited Talk by Dr. Sandro Pezzelle*

A Pipeline for the Creation of Multimodal Corpora from YouTube Videos

Nathan Dykes
Friedrich-Alexander-Universität Erlangen-Nürnberg
nathan.dykes@fau.de

Anna Wilson
University of Oxford
anna.wilson@area.ox.ac.uk

Peter Uhrig
ScaDS.AI Dresden/Leipzig
TU Dresden
peter.uhrig@tu-dresden.de

Abstract

This paper introduces an open-source pipeline for the creation of multimodal corpora from YouTube videos. It minimizes storage and bandwidth requirements, because the videos themselves need not be downloaded and can remain on YouTube's servers. It also minimizes processing requirements by using YouTube's automatically generated subtitles, thus avoiding a computationally expensive automatic speech recognition processing step. The pipeline combines standard tools and provides as its output a corpus file in the industry-standard vertical format used by many corpus managers. It is straightforwardly extensible with the addition of further levels of annotation and can be adapted to languages other than English.

1 Introduction

The analysis of multimodal communication has become mainstream in linguistic research in the past few decades, which results in a higher demand for multimodal corpus resources of ever-increasing size for more and more languages and varieties. While there are very good reasons for the manual creation of multimodal corpora when specific varieties are needed that usually occur beyond the public sphere, these approaches do not scale well due to the prohibitive cost of manual data collection, transcription and, possibly, annotation.

In corpus linguistics, a common approach for written corpora is using existing publications, often newspapers and other periodicals, or crawling web pages and social media. This is also possible for multimodal corpora, as illustrated by the NewsScape English Corpus (Uhrig, 2018, 2022), which is based on American TV News collected by the NewsScape project at UCLA and the related processing tools developed in the context of the Distributed Little Red Hen Lab (see e.g. Steen et al. (2018)). However, the processing pipeline is highly adapted to the peculiarities of the data, in particular the TV subtitles and metadata recorded, so it does not generalize well to other domains/datasets.

YouTube is a very interesting source for multimodal corpora for several reasons. One is the sheer number of videos hosted on the platform, and another is its breadth, which ranges from professionally produced and edited programs provided by broadcasters and other media outlets, via a variety of content created by more or less professional YouTubers, to content that bears witness to the relatively anarchic nature of the platform. Thus, YouTube is a treasure trove for the creators of multimodal corpora, who can select the videos they deem most representative of the language or variety they wish to study.

In this paper we introduce a processing pipeline for the creation of multimodal corpora from YouTube videos, making use of the automatically-generated subtitles provided by YouTube. We combine existing processing tools into a usable pipeline that needs as its input a set of YouTube URLs and provides as its output a corpus that can be imported directly into CQPweb, an open-source corpus manager (Hardie, 2012).

2 YouTube Captions as Corpus Data

As mentioned above, one of the most time-consuming and thus most expensive steps in the creation of multimodal corpora is the transcription of the spoken text. In TV broadcasts, subtitles are often created by humans, increasingly supported by automatic speech recognition (ASR) technology. YouTube allows content creators to provide their own subtitles to go with the videos, and some large broadcasters systematically provide the subtitles they broadcast for the YouTube recordings of the same program. However, measured by the scale of YouTube's size, this is a minuscule proportion of videos and, again, does not scale well. We will ignore these types of subtitles in the present pipeline and instead focus on YouTube's automatically gen-

Proceedings of the 1st Workshop on Linguistic Insights from and for Multimodal Language Processing, pages 1–5
September 22, 2023.

erated captions.

YouTube's automatic captioning system makes use of ASR to provide subtitles on videos in the following languages: Arabic, Dutch, English, French, German, Hindi, Indonesian, Italian, Japanese, Korean, Polish, Portuguese, Romanian, Russian, Spanish, Thai, Turkish, Ukrainian, and Vietnamese.[1] If a video is detected to be in one of these languages, YouTube will create automatic subtitles, which can be displayed on the video once the ASR process has finished. Content creators have to actively disable this if they do not want their video to be captioned, so most videos come with automatic captions. One of the major advantages of automatic captions compared to manually created captions as found on TV is that YouTube's captions come with relatively accurate timing information on the word level (if the right format is used – see next section) while the manual subtitles are usually presented line by line and tend to lag behind, especially on content that is (or was originally) broadcast live.

2.1 Downloads and Format(s)

YouTube downloads are a tricky business. Generally, YouTube as a for-profit company generating revenue through advertisement views has little interest in allowing bulk downloading of their data. On the other hand, there are legitimate uses of YouTube downloads that the open source community provides software for, which needs regular updates to keep up with the constant changes introduced by YouTube. In the first versions of the pipeline presented here, youtube-dl[2] was used to download the closed captions and write metadata files. The current version uses yt-dlp[3], which markets itself as "A youtube-dl fork with additional features and fixes". By default, youtube-dl and yt-dlp save downloaded files with the video title as the file name. Given that YouTube videos can contain almost arbitrary characters, not all of which are supported by all file systems, and given that video titles need not be unique, we use YouTube's 11-character video ID as the filename for the download and in all further processing.

YouTube stores its videos and subtitles in a variety of formats to provide the appropriate quality and formats depending on factors such as playback device, screen resolution/window size, and Internet connection speed. Audio and Video formats are not of interest for the purpose of the present paper, but the subtitle formats are. Some formats, for instance the popular SubRip format (.srt), only have line-level timing information and are thus not ideal for multimodal corpus building, because the corpus becomes more useful when every word has timing information associated with it. For this reason, the present pipeline uses the WebVTT format (.vtt), which at the time of implementation was the only format providing word-level timing information and a rough indication of ASR confidence encoded via the text color.[4]

In addition to the subtitles, our pipeline uses yt-dlp to download the info json file, which contains metadata about the video, e.g. upload date, uploader and channel, which are included in the corpora created.

2.2 Accuracy

To the best of our knowledge, YouTube does not publish statistics on the accuracy of the closed captions. Not surprisingly, the results are directly related to the quality of the audio signal, which is best in studio recordings of professional speakers of the standard language. This is in line with YouTube's own statement that "automatic captions might misrepresent the spoken content due to mispronunciations, accents, dialects, or background noise."[5] Furthermore, manual inspection showed that the reliability is severely reduced in languages such as Russian (where morphological forms are often incorrectly rendered even if the lemma is correctly recognized) or Turkish, where we see high error rates on the admittedly small samples tested. We assume that future versions of YouTube's captioning system will be based on Google's recent Universal Speech Model (Zhang et al., 2023), which should improve accuracy in lesser-resourced languages (and possibly add support for a much wider variety of languages).

3 NLP pipeline

Our pipeline is available for download at `https://github.com/RedHenLab/youtube_pipeline`. The various processing steps and their corresponding input and output data formats are given as an

[1] https://support.google.com/youtube/answer/6373554

[2] https://youtube-dl.org/

[3] https://github.com/yt-dlp/yt-dlp

[4] YouTube has since removed the text coloring from WebVTT subtitles and introduced the json3 format, which provides more fine-grained information on the ASR confidence. A version of our pipeline with json3 support will be made available by the start of KONVENS.

[5] https://support.google.com/youtube/answer/6373554

overview in Table 1. In principle, it is possible to add extensions or replace individual components of the pipeline at any given processing step as long as input and output formats remain intact.

3.1 Tokenisation

As YouTube provides the WebVTT format with word-level timing information, we have a type of implicit ("whitespace") tokenization to begin with (see however below), which might already be sufficient for certain applications. However, because our pipeline includes PoS tagging and syntactic parsing, we need to tokenize further to ensure compatibility with the downstream tools. For English, the vast majority of cases requiring additional tokenization can be solved with a regular expression that splits up contractions (*'s*|*'ve*|*'re*|*'d* etc.) before the apostrophe. In our tests, this approach was sufficient for more than 99% of videos. However, with larger corpora, the tokenization became increasingly challenging as several kinds of rare exceptions had to be addressed. Firstly, despite the captions usually appearing with no punctuation, individual files did occasionally contain punctuation marks which had most likely been introduced by manual modifications carried out by the content creator. Secondly, although typically each word is assigned a separate start time, some common expressions are treated as multi-word units, which means that they are displayed to the viewer as a chunk and thus have the same start timestamp (e.g. some instances of *a lot* or *a little*, repeated fillers like *uh hu* etc.). Thirdly, defaulting to setting token boundaries at common contraction or genitive markers occasionally produces errors. For instance, one of our videos contains the compound *bird's-eye-view*, where this ad-hoc tokenization would have produced the obviously nonsensical tokens *bird* and *'s-eye-view*. For these reasons, a more elaborate tokenization was necessary, for which we use SoMaJo (Proisl and Uhrig, 2016)[6] during our first processing step, where the text is converted to the CoNLL-U format that stores each token with the associated timestamps. Each token that is affected in this step is assigned to the same timestamps as the one original token in the .vtt file.

3.2 Punctuation Restoration

As mentioned in the section on tokenization, the automatic captions usually do not contain punctuation marks. This is problematic for NLP processing since the identification of phrase and sentence boundaries relies on this information. Standard NLP tools are trained on text with punctuation so that the accuracy of PoS tagging is reduced without it and syntactic parsing becomes downright impossible without sentence boundaries, which are typically derived from punctuation information. Not to mention the poor readability for researchers analyzing data without punctuation. It was therefore necessary to automatically insert punctuation marks in plausible positions. Fortunately, there are off-the-shelf solutions to this exact problem. We chose Alam et al. (2020)'s tool due to the promising results on different languages, and its rather straightforward usability out of the box.[7]

In its original version, this tool treats commas, colons and dashes as commas; and full stops, exclamation marks and semicolons as full stops. We fine-tuned the tool on the Brown Corpus family with slight tweaks to the original scripts, in order to also insert exclamation marks and dashes as separate categories, which we expect to be useful for analyses interested in fine-grained interactional phenomena. Given suitable training data, the process can easily be adapted to other languages. In this step, we also insert explicit sentence boundaries as a prerequisite for syntactic parsing.

3.3 Tagging, Parsing and Corpus Construction

In order to prepare the data for tagging, the punctuated text files are aligned with their original CONLL versions that contain the timestamp information. Newly inserted punctuation marks receive the same timestamp as the last token for which timing information is available. The data is then annotated for PoS, lemma and other morpho-syntactic features with UDPipe 1 (Straka et al., 2016), which was selected because it supports a large number of the languages for which YouTube provides automatic captions. Since we use standard CoNLL-U files as input and output, it is comparably easy to plug in a different library if needed.

4 CQPweb

The tagged and parsed files are then converted to vertical text files (.vrt), which is the standard input format for the Corpus Workbench (Evert and

[6] Although SoMaJo was only developed for English and German, it has been successfully applied to other languages.

[7] The original tool can be found at `https://github.com/xashru/punctuation-restoration`. Our pipeline uses a fork of this repository that is linked in the README.

Processing Step	Input Data	Output Data
YouTube download	Text file with YouTube URLs	WebVTT subtitles and info-JSON metadata file
Subtitle extraction and tokenization	WebVTT subtitles	CoNLL-U input for NLP
Raw Text extraction	CoNLL-U	plain text
Punctuation restoration	plain text	plain text with punctuation marks and sentence boundaries
Merging punctuation restoration results	CoNLL-U and plain text with punctuation marks and sentence boundaries	CoNLL-U
NLP with UDPipe	CoNLL-U	CoNLL-U
creation of corpus files	CoNLL-U and info-JSON metadata file	vertical file for each video
corpus aggregation	vertical files for each video	one vertical file for the entire corpus

Table 1: Overview of processing steps with input and output data

Hardie, 2011) and, by extension, CQPweb (Hardie, 2012), which we currently use to conduct our analyses. In this step of the pipeline, the annotated files are combined with relevant metadata from the info-JSON files associated with each video. Currently, we extract information on the uploader, the channel, the video title, the upload date, and the duration in seconds. Timestamps are added in separate columns so that we can jump directly to the right position in the video for every word in the corpus.

CQPweb is a browser-based frontend to the Corpus Workbench. As compared to other readily available corpus tools, CQPweb has several advantages which make it particularly suitable for our research endeavours. Firstly, it allows for very flexible queries combining arbitrary levels of annotation; thus allowing us e.g. to search for combinations of linguistic and gestural features. Secondly, its core functionality can be enhanced through custom plugins and visualizations, which we use to link to the YouTube videos in the right position.

5 Conclusion

The pipeline we presented here enables corpus linguists to create multimodal corpora from YouTube in a straightforward way. The user needs to provide a text file with YouTube links, which can be links to individual videos or to entire YouTube channels, which will then be downloaded. After the download, all successfully retrieved subtitle files will be processed by the NLP pipeline, which will output a single .vrt file and an accompanying list of attributes for import into CQPweb. In addition, due to the open and simple formats used, the pipeline can be extended with further annotation levels, e.g. based on automatic prosodic or computer vision analysis, which can be added as extra columns in the vertical file. Together with the custom visualization for video playback and the download plugin provided for CQPweb, a fully functional multimodal corpus is at the linguist's fingertips.[8]

Limitations

The full pipeline presented in this paper is currently only available for auto-generated subtitles in English, but an earlier (and simpler) multilingual pipeline (whitespace tokenization, no punctuation restoration, briefly presented in Uhrig (2022)) has been successfully applied to a Russian-language YouTube dataset.

Ethics Statement

Researchers using our pipeline are faced with three ethics questions. The first concerns their relationship to the video producer and the people recorded in the video. Are any personal rights violated by including the video in question in a corpus? The second question is in their relationship to the legal requirements and codes of conduct when collecting data, e.g. questions of copyright, where there are exemptions for academic research in many but

[8] See Uhrig et al. (2023) for the use of this pipeline in a larger research project and its application in a case study.

not all jurisdictions. The third is the relationship between the researcher and YouTube as the content provider, whose terms and conditions may restrict certain types of automated downloads in certain jurisdictions. Researchers are solely responsible for their own use of this pipeline.

Acknowledgements

The research presented in this paper was made possible by generous funding provided by the Deutsche Forschungsgemeinschaft (project number 468466485) and the Arts and Humanities Research Council (grant reference AH/W010720/1) to the second and the last author. The authors gratefully acknowledge the scientific support and HPC resources provided by the Erlangen National High Performance Computing Center (NHR@FAU) of the Friedrich-Alexander-Universität Erlangen-Nürnberg (FAU) under the NHR project b105dc to the second author. NHR funding is provided by federal and Bavarian state authorities. NHR@FAU hardware is partially funded by the German Research Foundation (DFG) – 440719683. The authors also gratefully acknowledge funding by the Defence Science and Technology Laboratory, Ministry of Defence, awarded to a project led by the second author.

References

Tanvirul Alam, Akib Khan, and Firoj Alam. 2020. Punctuation restoration using transformer models for high- and low-resource languages. In *Proceedings of the Sixth Workshop on Noisy User-generated Text (W-NUT 2020)*, pages 132–142.

Stefan Evert and Andrew Hardie. 2011. Twenty-first century corpus workbench: Updating a query architecture for the new millennium. In *Proceedings of the Corpus Linguistics 2011 conference*.

Andrew Hardie. 2012. Cqpweb—combining power, flexibility and usability in a corpus analysis tool. *International journal of corpus linguistics*, 17(3):380–409.

Thomas Proisl and Peter Uhrig. 2016. Somajo: State-of-the-art tokenization for german web and social media texts. In *Proceedings of the 10th Web as Corpus Workshop*, pages 57–62.

Francis F. Steen, Anders Hougaard, Jungseock Joo, Inés Olza, Cristóbal Pagán Cánovas, Anna Pleshakova, Soumya Ray, Peter Uhrig, Javier Valenzuela, Jacek Woźny, and Mark Turner. 2018. Toward an infrastructure for data-driven multimodal communication research. *Linguistics Vanguard*, 4(1).

Milan Straka, Jan Hajic, and Jana Straková. 2016. Udpipe: trainable pipeline for processing conll-u files performing tokenization, morphological analysis, pos tagging and parsing. In *Proceedings of the Tenth International Conference on Language Resources and Evaluation (LREC'16)*, pages 4290–4297.

Peter Uhrig. 2018. NewsScape and the Distributed Little Red Hen Lab – A digital infrastructure for the large-scale analysis of TV broadcasts. In *Anglistentag 2017 in Regensburg: Proceedings. Proceedings of the Conference of the German Association of University Teachers of English*, pages 99–114, Trier. Wissenschaftlicher Verlag Trier.

Peter Uhrig. 2022. *Large-Scale Multimodal Corpus Linguistics – The Big Data Turn*. Habilitation thesis, Friedrich Alexander Universität Erlangen-Nürnberg.

Peter Uhrig, Elinor Payne, Irina Pavlova, Ilya Burenko, Nathan Dykes, Mary Baltazani, Evie Burrows, Scott Hale, Philip Torr, and Anna Wilson. 2023. Studying time conceptualisation via speech, prosody, and hand gesture: Interweaving manual and computational methods of analysis. In *Proceedings of the 8th Gesture and Speech in Interaction Conference*.

Yu Zhang, Wei Han, James Qin, Yongqiang Wang, Ankur Bapna, Zhehuai Chen, Nanxin Chen, Bo Li, Vera Axelrod, Gary Wang, Zhong Meng, Ke Hu, Andrew Rosenberg, Rohit Prabhavalkar, Daniel S. Park, Parisa Haghani, Jason Riesa, Ginger Perng, Hagen Soltau, Trevor Strohman, Bhuvana Ramabhadran, Tara Sainath, Pedro Moreno, Chung-Cheng Chiu, Johan Schalkwyk, Françoise Beaufays, and Yonghui Wu. 2023. Google usm: Scaling automatic speech recognition beyond 100 languages.

Multi-Modal Learning Application - Support Language Learners with NLP Techniques and Eye-Tracking

Robert Geislinger, Ali Ebrahimi Pourasad, Deniz Gül, Daniel Djahangir, Seid Muhie Yimam, Steffen Remus, Chris Biemann
Language Technology Group, Universität Hamburg, Germany
firstname.lastname@uni-hamburg.de

Abstract

This paper presents a framework consisting of an iPad application and an NLP pipeline, designed to assist non-native speakers in learning English as a second language. The application provides beginner-level texts, which are augmented by contextual images to facilitate natural learning. The multi-modal iOS application can be fully controlled by employing eye-tracking components, aiming to enhance the reading experience by highlighting relevant parts of an image when the user naturally focuses a particular and potentially complex word. Moreover, this eye-tracking feature offers accessibility for individuals with physical disabilities.

1 Introduction

In our interconnected world, learning a new language is increasingly necessary for social, professional, or political purposes. Language acquisition is challenging, even though various supporting methods are available. For infants, parents often associate object names through pointing. Self-study of a language can involve using educational applications or engaging with media in the language. For instance, learning through activities like reading subtitles while watching films can be easier than solely relying on reading educational texts (Danan, 1992). This technique of learning, where individuals are presented with multiple representations, e.g., text and image, is known as multimodal learning. It has been shown in studies that this technique enhances learning comprehension (Wang et al., 2022).

This project offers a multi-modal learning application, which can be managed by tracking the users eye movement. It facilitates natural language learning by combining suitable sentences with related images. The target users of the application are beginners and individuals with motor difficulties, making it challenging for them to use touch-based applications. The application can be used independently by individuals or provided by organizations and educational institutions. The machine learning models used for the identifying a word and highlighting the respective object in an image are trained on English, but are easily exchangeable for other languages. The following user flow serves as an example of how the application can be used:

Upon launching the application, the user is presented with a selection of topics to choose from. After selecting a topic, a sentence is presented with a contextually fitting image. This could be a sentence about motorsports, accompanied by an image of a Formula One car that is relevant to the chosen topic. The NLP pipeline has previously identified potentially complex words which might be hard to learn or understand. While the user is reading the text, the eye-tracking component tracks the eye movement. If the user looks at a complex word, it is highlighted within the text and the image. E.g., if 'wheel' is identified as a complex word in the sentence, the wheels of the car in the image will be highlighted when the user looks at the word.

2 Related Work

The term Mobile Assisted Language Learning (MALL) was coined by Chinnery (2006) and describes the learning of languages with mobile devices. MALL applications can encompass a multimodal approach including face-to-face communication (Vigliocco et al., 2014) and the use of images and texts (Schneider et al., 2021). The popularity of MALL applications is evident, as seen in platforms like Duolingo[1], which has over 300 million users (Shortt et al., 2021). Language learning applications can support learners and enhance their speaking and critical thinking skills (Kusmaryani et al., 2019).

Eye-tracking is a method that tracks eye position

[1] https://www.duolingo.com

Proceedings of the 1st Workshop on Linguistic Insights from and for Multimodal Language Processing, pages 6–11
September 22, 2023. ©2023 Association for Computational Linguistics

Figure 1: Menu View: Topic overview. Selection by touch and eye-tracking.

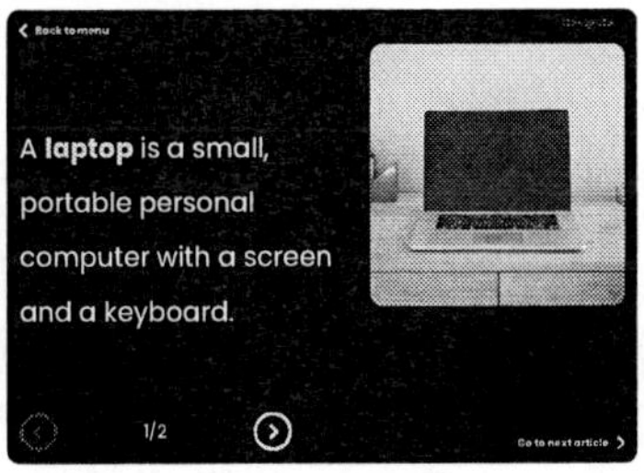

Figure 2: Reading View: A text about 'laptop' with the focus word laptop and a image about laptops.

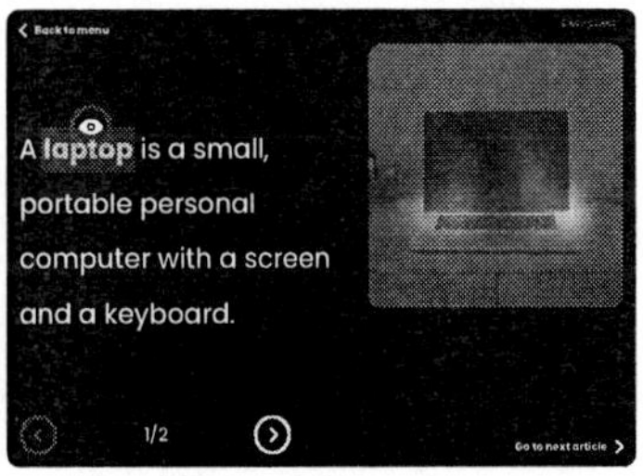

Figure 3: Reading View: The user looks at the word 'laptop which is highlighted in the image and text.

to identify an individual's gaze, such as images on a computer screen or real-world traffic signs. It has applications in psychology (Rahal and Fiedler, 2019; Li and Pollatsek, 2020), medicine (Harezlak and Kasprowski, 2018), and advertising (Lohse and Wu, 2001). Several eye-tracking solutions that differ in their accuracy and expense. Specialized eye-tracking hardware is often costly and used in laboratory environments. These devices are head-mounted (Cognolato et al., 2018) or use a fixed, steady camera in front of the user (Sharaev et al., 2021). Accessible eye-tracking for the masses as in the presented work can be achieved by utilizing inexpensive and commonly used consumer hardware, such as webcams or mobile devices (Papoutsaki, 2015). The main difference is that consumer hardware is generally less accurate, although the accuracy is improving with the evolution of consumer hardware such as mobile phones (Krafka et al., 2016). Technologies such as eye-tracking mostly benefits impaired people, but not exclusively (Elliott et al., 2019; Milde et al., 2021).

State-of-the-art computer vision models can predict unfamiliar concepts alongside predefined object categories by learning on datasets comprising ofnumerous images and their corresponding textual descriptions (Radford et al., 2021). By extracting visual and textual features from the input data and comparing them using a similarity metric, such models can determine the degree to which a given text input is related to a particular image. Using the approach, one can find the best matching image to a given text from a database of images (Salvador et al., 2017). Models for finding and highlighting parts of the image depending on a query are also available (Schneider and Biemann, 2022). New possibilities arise, like forecasting image content, but these models demand substantial computational resources for training and prediction, as well as extensive datasets to attain reasonable results (Radford et al., 2021).

3 System design

The system architecture consists of two main components: the frontend and the backend. The frontend is an iOS application that processes touch and eye-tracking inputs, while also displaying the preprocessed texts and images. The backend is used to process text-aligned image datasets and to extract important meta information, which is then used to present the user.

3.1 Frontend

An iOS application for the iPad was chosen as the frontend for the project due to access to Apple's augmented reality library, RealityKit[2], which provides eye and facial tracking capabilities and can generate screen coordinates of the user's current focus. The generated coordinates were found to be imprecise for accurate tracking, possibly because the library's coordinate system lacks calibration based on the user's distance and orientation to the device. A common practice to calibrate eye-tracking systems is to show calibration dots for the user to look at (Gunawardena et al., 2022). When the user opens the app, a custom calibration process starts to calculate more precise coordinates. The user gazes at four corner circles displayed on the screen to establish reference points. This step enhances the library's coordinate system, improving the accuracy of tracking the user's eye gaze. The user's viewpoint is represented by an eye pictogram within a circle, which is controlled by the user's eye movement, similar to a mouse pointer. This can be seen in Figure 3, where the eye pictogram is positioned above the word 'laptop'.

After calibration, the Menu View displays options to select a topic, as shown in Figure 1. Once a

[2]https://developer.apple.com/augmented-reality/realitykit/

topic is selected, the user is directed to the Reading View. Figure 2 illustrates the Reading View with a sentence about laptops, accompanied by an image that appropriately visualizes the sentence and its context. While reading, the application highlights the word 'laptop' in bold letters. Whenever the user's eye focuses on the word, it gets highlighted both in the sentence and in the image. This allows the user to learn the word intuitively without having to look up its definition. Figure 3 provides an example of this. After completing a sentence, the user can either learn more sentences within the same topic or move on to a different topic.

In order to create a functional eye-tracking system, several factors need to be taken into account. This is essential for accurately tracking the user's eyes and ultimately influencing their interaction with the application. The system utilizes the iPad's front camera, which has lower image quality than the rear camera. This introduces uncertainty due to lower resolution and issues related to low-light conditions. To overcome this uncertainty, it is necessary to optimize and mitigate other aspects of the eye-tracking system. When the iPad is in landscape mode, the camera is positioned on the side instead of the center, leading to more accurate eye-tracking on the side facing the camera. To get feedback on the tracking, five volunteers were asked to test the application on an iPad Mini 6th generation and iPad Pro 5 generation in a small pilot study. The different technical details of the devices, such as screen size, camera and processor, made it possible to look at various aspects. The users have reported problems with tracking on both devices and orientations. However, tracking consistently worked better when the elements were placed on the side closer to the camera and larger elements could be focused better than smaller elements. To address this issue, precise tracking elements, such as educational texts in Reading View, are positioned on the side facing the camera. In addition, elements as buttons and texts, are enlarged to help avoid collisions with the user's focused eye position during tracking. User head movement can significantly reduce eye-tracking system accuracy.

The system recalibrates the coordinate system if the predicted viewport is close to a button. It is assumed that the eye-tracking mechanism is imprecise, and the user is fixating at the center of the button. The offset between the button's center and the tracked point is calculated to adjust the coordinate system. To prevent accidental button activation, the user must gaze at the button for three seconds. The recalibration process is performed multiple times within the three-second period, with the ring around the pointer acting as a progress bar. After this period, the button's command is executed. This mechanism is also used to initiate the recalibration process when the user begins reading a text. In this application, users read texts from the top left corner to the bottom right. When the user's eyes are tracked near the first word, the recalibration is applied.

3.2 Backend

Figure 4 shows an overview of the preprocessing NLP pipeline, which filters the text documents and enriches them with corresponding descriptive images. The pipeline is based on Wang et al. (2022). The text dataset is a collection of documents from the Simple English Wikipedia[3]. This dataset covers a wide range of topics, including animals, food, cities and other subjects, making it diverse. The pipeline tokenizes the documents into sentences and processes them independently. First, the pipeline identifies complex words in a sentence, primarily those that exceed the language classification level B1 according to the Common European Framework of Reference for Languages (CEFR). For example, the word 'minute' in the context of time is classified as A1 (Beginner) and 'a minute amount of fuel' as quantification as C2 (Proficiency English). This classification is performed using the complex word identification algorithm developed by Srivastava (2022). The algorithm utilizes a sequential model developed by Rei (2017) that incorporates hand-engineered features, along with word embeddings, to classify complex words based on their context.

In addition to identifying complex words, depictable words are also identified. A word is considered highly depictable if it can be easily visualized, such as the word 'dog,' which represents a physical entity. On the other hand, the word 'creativity' is difficult to visualize because it represents an abstract concept without a concrete visual representation (Hessel et al., 2018).

First, the annotated image dataset, MSCOCO (Lin et al., 2014), is used to initialize the algorithm. Then the algorithm calculates the concreteness scores for the words in the annotations. If the

[3]https://simple.wikipedia.org

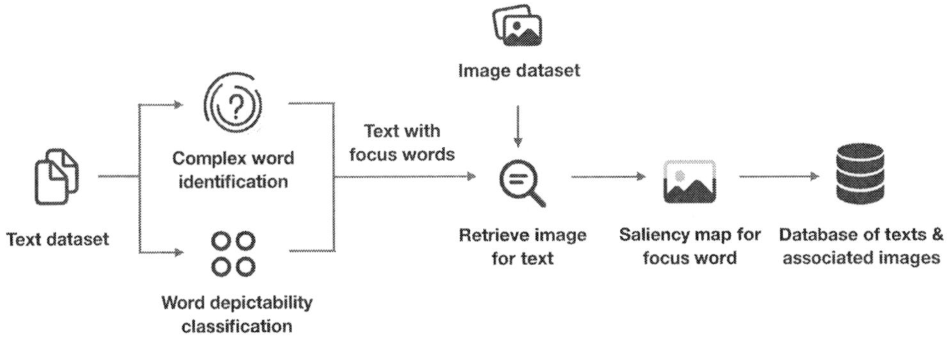

Figure 4: The preprocessing NLP pipeline, which enriches text with context-fitting images.

score exceeds a threshold of 50, as tested by Hessel et al. (2018), and the corresponding word is a noun, it is considered depictable. Once the depictable items are identified from the image dataset annotations, they are mapped to their corresponding words in the textual dataset, if those words exist.

After the complexity and representability classification, only those words that satisfy both criteria are considered. These complex and depictable words are referred to as 'focus words' (Wang et al., 2022) which require explanation and can be represented visually to facilitate learning. In the end, only sentences that contain at least one focus word are retained in the text dataset.

Next, each sentence in the filtered text dataset is matched with a relevant image that showcases the contextualized focus words. This step is crucial as words can possess multiple meanings based on their context. For example, the word 'bank' can refer to a shore in a river or a financial institution. To find relevant images, the CLIP model[4] (Radford et al., 2021) calculates the cosine similarity between images and words or sentences. The image dataset used is MSCOCO[5], which is also utilized for the word depictability classification. An image is considered similar to a sentence or word, if the similarity value calculated by CLIP exceeds a threshold of 4.0. Following the approach by Wang et al. (2022), sentences are only processed further, if there are five similar candidate images. The most similar candidate image to the focus words is selected as the associated image for a sentence. If none of the five candidate images show similarity to any focus word in the sentence, the sentence is excluded.

To highlight the focus words in the image, mini-CLIP[6] is utilized for visualization. The generated saliency maps are superimposed on the original image shown in Figure 2 and Figure 3.

Once all sentences in a text document are processed throughout the processing steps, the text document and its retrieved images are stored in the database. The frontend can then access all the topics, sentences, and accompanying images from the database through a REST API.

4 Conclusion

The goal of this project was to support novice language learners by developing an educational iPad application. The application designed combines modern NLP techniques and eye-tracking technology enabling a multi-modal learning experience with beginner-friendly texts and accompanying images that help illustrate the content. The integrated eye-tracker analyzes the users' reading behavior and enhances their reading experience by highlighting relevant parts of images. Furthermore, eye-tracking enables individuals with physical disabilities to access the application. One of the major challenges encountered was implementing eye tracking on the iPad. Despite the efforts, improving the accuracy and stability of the eye-tracking system is necessary for it to be considered user-friendly. The main issues are the low image quality of the iPad's camera and ensuring the users's head stability during use. To address these challenges, one could explore alternative eye-tracking algorithms or contemplate integrating an external camera in the future to improve image quality.

As an alternative to relying solely on datasets, one could leverage AI generation tools such as Stable Diffusion (Rombach et al., 2022) or GPT-4 (OpenAI, 2023), which have the ability to create

[4]https://github.com/openai/CLIP
[5]https://cocodataset.org
[6]https://github.com/HendrikStrobelt/miniClip

images based on input descriptions.

The next step in this research should involve conducting user studies with language learners to quantitatively evaluate the effectiveness of using eye-tracking technology to highlight objects in contextual images during the learning process. How much users benefit from contextual images compared to users without this support would be part of an evaluation study. Also a usability study should be carried out with the aim of adapting the application to the needs of the users in the best possible way.

The project is openly available under a permissive Apache v2 License[7].

5 Acknowledgments

Funded by the Federal Ministry of Education and Research (BMBF) and the Free and Hanseatic City of Hamburg under the Excellence Strategy of the Federal Government and the Länder.

6 Limitations

The models utilized in the NLP pipeline have been specifically trained for the English language. While the pipeline can potentially be adapted to other languages with appropriate datasets, the availability of such datasets remains a challenge. The hard filtering process employed during dataset creation limits the languages for which fitting datasets are readily accessible. This restriction poses a barrier to deploying the pipeline for languages with small available datasets, as it would require significant efforts to collect and curate appropriate data for training.

The application relies on a server for its functionality, which poses a limitation in terms of scalability and availability. Running the application without a server connection is currently not possible, hindering its use in offline environments. Future improvements could explore alternative approaches, such as client-side implementations or optimizing server dependencies to minimize their impact on the application's usability.

Another important consideration is the computational power required to preprocess the data using the pipeline. The image and text data need to be processed beforehand to achieve satisfying results, which necessitates a server with sufficient computational capabilities.

[7] `https://github.com/Alienmaster/MultimodalLearningIOSApp`

7 Ethical Aspects

The ethical aspects of a language learning application with eye-tracking for disabled people revolve around ensuring inclusivity and equal opportunities for individuals with disabilities. The application prioritize user privacy and data security, ensuring that the eye-tracking data is not collected, shared or exploited. Even though the application was developed with a focus on eye-tracking, it is also fully usable with touch to give the user a choice. By providing the complete software and source code, including all models and data sets, users and developers can trace the use of the data within the application. If eye-tracking data is later used for optimisation purposes, sufficient safeguards must be in place to protect the security of the users' data. Due to the complete open-source approach, there are still no costs for either the user or the developer.

References

George M Chinnery. 2006. Going to the MALL: Mobile assisted language learning. *Language learning & technology*, 10(1):9–16.

Matteo Cognolato, Manfredo Atzori, and Henning Müller. 2018. Head-mounted eye gaze tracking devices: An overview of modern devices and recent advances. *Journal of Rehabilitation and Assistive Technologies Engineering*, 5(13):1–13.

Martine Danan. 1992. Reversed Subtitling and Dual Coding Theory: New Directions for Foreign Language Instruction. *Language Learning*, 42(4):497–527.

Michael A Elliott, Henrique Malvar, Lindsey L Maassel, Jon Campbell, Harish Kulkarni, Irina Spiridonova, Noelle Sophy, Jay Beavers, Ann Paradiso, Chuck Needham, et al. 2019. Eye-controlled, power wheelchair performs well for ALS patients. *Muscle & nerve*, 60(5):513–519.

Nishan Gunawardena, Jeewani Anupama Ginige, and Bahman Javadi. 2022. Eye-tracking Technologies in Mobile Devices Using Edge Computing: A Systematic Review. *ACM Computing Surveys*, 55(8):1–33.

Katarzyna Harezlak and Pawel Kasprowski. 2018. Application of eye tracking in medicine: A survey, research issues and challenges. *Computerized Medical Imaging and Graphics*, 65:176–190. Advances in Biomedical Image Processing.

Jack Hessel, David Mimno, and Lillian Lee. 2018. Quantifying the visual concreteness of words and topics in multimodal datasets. In *Proceedings of the 2018 Conference of the North American Chapter of the Association for Computational Linguistics: Human Language Technologies, Volume 1 (Long Papers)*, pages 2194–2205, New Orleans, Louisiana. Association for Computational Linguistics.

Kyle Krafka, Aditya Khosla, Petr Kellnhofer, Harini Kannan, Suchendra Bhandarkar, Wojciech Matusik, and Antonio Torralba. 2016. Eye Tracking for Everyone. In *Proceedings of 2016 IEEE Conference on Computer Vision and Pattern Recognition (CVPR)*, pages 2176–2184, Las Vegas, USA.

W Kusmaryani, B Musthafa, and Pupung Purnawarman. 2019. The influence of mobile applications on students' speaking skill and critical thinking in English language learning. In *Journal of Physics: Conference Series*, volume 1193, pages 1–6, Bogor, Indonesia.

Xingshan Li and Alexander Pollatsek. 2020. An Integrated Model of Word Processing and Eye-Movement Control During Chinese Reading. *Psychological Review*, 127(6):1139–1162.

Tsung-Yi Lin, Michael Maire, Serge Belongie, James Hays, Pietro Perona, Deva Ramanan, Piotr Dollár, and C. Lawrence Zitnick. 2014. Microsoft COCO: Common Objects in Context. In *In Proceedings of European conference on computer vision (ECCV)*, pages 740–755, Zurich, Switzerland.

Gerald L Lohse and DJ Wu. 2001. Eye Movement Patterns on Chinese Yellow Pages Advertising. *Electronic Markets*, 11(2):87–96.

Benjamin Milde, Robert Geislinger, Irina Lindt, and Timo Baumann. 2021. Open Source Automatic Lecture Subtitling. In *Proceedings of Electronic Speech Signal Processing 2021 (ESSV)*, pages 128–134, Berlin, Germany.

OpenAI. 2023. GPT-4 Technical Report.

Alexandra Papoutsaki. 2015. Scalable Webcam Eye Tracking by Learning from User Interactions. In *Proceedings of the 33rd Annual ACM Conference Extended Abstracts on Human Factors in Computing Systems 2015 (CHI)*, pages 219–222, Seoul, Republic of Korea.

Alec Radford, Jong Wook Kim, Chris Hallacy, Aditya Ramesh, Gabriel Goh, Sandhini Agarwal, Girish Sastry, Amanda Askell, Pamela Mishkin, Jack Clark, et al. 2021. Learning Transferable Visual Models From Natural Language Supervision. In *In Proceedings of International Conference on Machine Learning (PMLR)*, volume 139, pages 8748–8763, online.

Rima-Maria Rahal and Susann Fiedler. 2019. Understanding cognitive and affective mechanisms in social psychology through eye-tracking. *Journal of Experimental Social Psychology*, 85:1–14.

Marek Rei. 2017. Semi-supervised Multitask Learning for Sequence Labeling. In *Proceedings of the 55th Annual Meeting of the Association for Computational Linguistics (Volume 1: Long Papers)*, pages 2121–2130, Vancouver, BC, Canada.

Robin Rombach, Andreas Blattmann, Dominik Lorenz, Patrick Esser, and Bjorn Ommer. 2022. High-Resolution Image Synthesis with Latent Diffusion Models. In *Proceedings of the 2022 IEEE/CVF Conference on Computer Vision and Pattern Recognition (CVPR)*, pages 10674–10685, New Orleans, LO, USA. IEEE Computer Society.

Amaia Salvador, Nicholas Hynes, Yusuf Aytar, Javier Marin, Ferda Ofli, Ingmar Weber, and Antonio Torralba. 2017. Learning cross-modal embeddings for cooking recipes and food images. In *Proceedings of 2017 IEEE Conference on Computer Vision and Pattern Recognition (CVPR)*, pages 3020–3028, Honolulu, HI, USA.

Florian Schneider, Özge Alaçam, Xintong Wang, and Chris Biemann. 2021. Towards multi-modal text-image retrieval to improve human reading. In *Proceedings of the 2021 Conference of the North American Chapter of the Association for Computational Linguistics: Student Research Workshop*, Online. Association for Computational Linguistics.

Florian Schneider and Chris Biemann. 2022. Golden Retriever: A Real-Time Multi-Modal Text-Image Retrieval System with the Ability to Focus. In *Proceedings of the 45th International ACM SIGIR Conference on Research and Development in Information Retrieval*, pages 3245–3250, New York, NY, United States.

Maxim Sharaev, Svetlana Sushchinskaya, Valentina Bachurina, George Taranov, Evgeny Burnaev, and Marie Arsalidou. 2021. Machine learning, eye movements and mathematical problem solving. *Journal of Vision (jov)*, 21(9):2397–2397.

Mitchell Shortt, Shantanu Tilak, Irina Kuznetcova, Bethany Martens, and Babatunde Akinkuolie. 2021. Gamification in mobile-assisted language learning: A systematic review of Duolingo literature from public release of 2012 to early 2020. *Computer Assisted Language Learning*, pages 1–38.

Ankit Srivastava. 2022. Complex Word Identification for Language Learners. Master's thesis, Universität Hamburg, Hamburg, Germany.

Gabriella Vigliocco, Pamela Perniss, and David Vinson. 2014. Language as a multimodal phenomenon: implications for language learning, processing and evolution. *Philosophical Transactions of the Royal Society B: Biological Sciences*, 369(1651):1–7.

Xintong Wang, Florian Schneider, Özge Alaçam, Prateek Chaudhury, and Chris Biemann. 2022. MOTIF: Contextualized Images for Complex Words to Improve Human Reading. In *Proceedings of the Thirteenth Language Resources and Evaluation Conference (LREC)*, pages 2468–2477, Marseille, France.

Context matters: evaluation of target and context features on variation of object naming

Nikolai Ilinykh and **Simon Dobnik**
Centre for Linguistic Theory and Studies in Probability (CLASP),
Department of Philosophy, Linguistics and Theory of Science (FLoV),
University of Gothenburg, Sweden
name.surname@gu.se

Abstract

Semantic underspecification in language poses significant difficulties for models in the field of referring expression generation. This challenge becomes particularly pronounced in setups, where models need to learn from multiple modalities and their combinations. Given that different contexts require different levels of language adaptability, models face difficulties in capturing the varying degrees of specificity. To address this issue, we focus on the task of object naming and evaluate various context representations to identify the ones that enable a computational model to effectively capture human variation in object naming. Once we identify the set of useful features, we combine them in search of the optimal combination that leads to a higher correlation with humans and brings us closer to developing a standard referring expression generation model that is aware of variation in naming. The results of our study demonstrate that achieving human-like naming variation requires the model to possess extensive knowledge about the target object from multiple modalities, as well as scene-level context representations. We believe that our findings contribute to the development of more sophisticated models of referring expression generation that aim to replicate *human-like* behaviour and performance. Our code is available at https://github.com/GU-CLASP/object-naming-in-context.

1 Introduction

The adaptability of human language presents a significant challenge for computational modelling, as it relies on both external contextual factors and internal personal beliefs and goals of the language users. The significance of the intents and goals cannot be overstated, as they dictate the specific choice of referring expressions and object descriptions (van Miltenburg, 2017; Ilinykh et al., 2018; Alikhani and Stone, 2019; Baltaretu et al., 2019; Mädebach et al., 2022). Furthermore, these choices can vary depending on the specific task or the absence thereof. Put simply, language continues to evolve and adapt, while existing models are typically trained to generalise. Evaluating such systems proves hard, as evaluation metrics typically assume a single optimal solution, disregarding other valid alternatives (Kreiss et al., 2022). As variation in language arises due to different levels of underspecification between language units (words) (Pezzelle, 2023), addressing this problem brings valuable insights into understanding the effects of the task, contexts and how their interplay can be modelled.

But what is the "task"? And how do we define "context"? A task-oriented language use is often understood through the prism of human-human interaction, where communicative goals are important (Brennan and Clark, 1996). During these interactions, a shared understanding, known as a common ground, is established to optimise communication (Stalnaker, 1978). What ends up being in common ground is dependent on the task, and the importance of tasks and intents for modelling language has been emphasised in many recent proposals to language grounding (Andreas, 2022; Schlangen, 2022; Giulianelli, 2022; Fried et al., 2023). In contrast, language can be used to simply describe objects in the world with an intent to **identify** them. These intents are typically determined by the set of instructions provided to a human e.g. "describe an image" (Lin et al., 2014). In doing so, we perform *the object identification task* which is a communicative act, albeit a highly specific one.

The intent to simply describe things without a specific communicative goal has been one of the traditional tasks in the field of natural language generation (NLG). As referring is an important aspect of human communication (Frank and Goodman, 2012), much computational work has focused on building automatic referring expression generation systems (Krahmer and van Deemter, 2012). The primary goal of referring expression generation is

Proceedings of the 1st Workshop on Linguistic Insights from and for Multimodal Language Processing, pages 12–24
September 22, 2023.

to produce a text in natural language that identifies a target object within a given context (Reiter and Dale, 2000) by making the object uniquely identifiable from the distractors. In the absence of the communicative intent, the definition of "given context" becomes extremely important as it directly influences referring (Schüz et al., 2023). **Visual context**, for instance, plays a crucial role in determining the content of the referring expression. This can be exemplified by multiple variables such as naturalness of the scenes where the target object appears (van Deemter et al., 2006; Mitchell et al., 2013; Kazemzadeh et al., 2014) or the presence of visual distractors and their position relative to the target object (Graf et al., 2016) and the typicality of the visual context as a whole (Gualdoni et al., 2022a,b,c). But visual context is not the only context available in the task of referring. Humans also rely on their knowledge of the world when describing things, and their **background knowledge** influences the choice of referring given a specific visual context (Dale and Viethen, 2009). In fact, the use of various names to refer to a single entity stems from the fact that different speakers tackle underspecification in different ways. Humans use given context to fill in the missing information, but they do so differently based on individual perspectives. Therefore, investigating the effect of different contexts on the naming variation and capturing human behaviour in models is beneficial for developing a better REG architecture.

This study addresses two challenges: (i) existing models of referring are simply not learning to approximate possible names for entities and (ii) it is hard to generate a correct name if the level of semantic underspecification is high. As underspecification is correlated in humans with variation, we assume that the models that approximate human behaviour should be equally "confused" as humans when generating descriptions and should produce the same variation. For a model that is behaving this way we can be sure that the variation is due to the way they capture semantic knowledge and context sensitivity rather than the noise (e.g., better performance on more frequent labels). **Our primary questions** are as follows: what is the set of features that enables computational model to closely capture the variation observed in human object naming? Can we combine such features to get closer to a REG model that can capture human-like object naming?

To address the questions outlined above, we investigate the effects that different context representations have on the model that is tasked with predicting an object name. We use CLIP (Radford et al., 2021) to encode different context representations and train a simple classifier to predict target object names using the Many Names dataset (Silberer et al., 2020b,a). We specifically examine how different features influence model's ability to capture human object naming variation. Through the comparison of the model's performance with humans across various metrics, we identify features that assist the model in making more valid and contextually motivated approximations of naming variation, reminiscent of human behaviour. We then combine different features and examine their fit for capturing naming variation. Our results demonstrate that the model that captures contextual sensitivity of object naming well (be it language or vision or both) is a good approximation of human knowledge and behaviour. We note that, unlike Silberer et al. (2020b), we are testing how different types of knowledge contribute to naming variation rather than building or evaluating object naming models. While Silberer et al. (2020b) also focus on typicality and whether the name is the top one or an alternative one in naming, we are interested in individual variation and the effects of context representations on the "distortions" of such typicality.

2 Problem formulation

2.1 Dataset

As our dataset, we use the Many Names dataset (Silberer et al., 2020b) as it provides a suitable testbed for studying naming variation. This dataset stands out from other language-and-vision data collections that can be used for studying naming variation (Mitchell et al., 2013; Kazemzadeh et al., 2014; Plummer et al., 2015; Yu et al., 2016; Krishna et al., 2017) due to its high number of name types per object and alignment between names and objects. This way we can directly study the variation in reference to entities. The dataset was created by picking a single target object per image based on annotated data from Visual Genome (Krishna et al., 2017). Next, name annotations for each object were collected from multiple crowd-workers[1]. There are on average 36 name tokens per object in Many Names, and their name types are sorted based on the frequency of being used to refer to

[1]For details, see Silberer et al. (2020a).

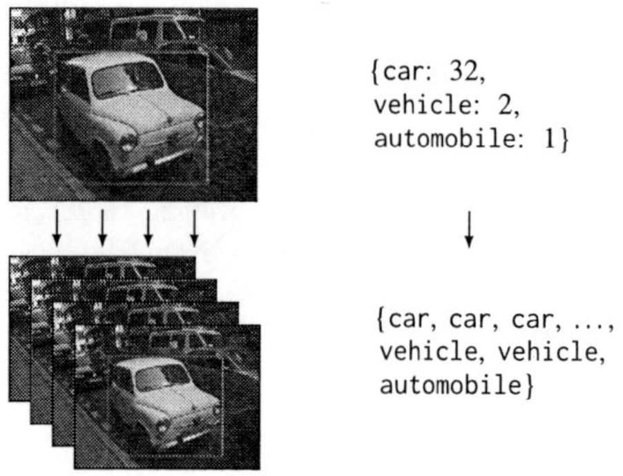

Figure 1: Dissecting the Many Names dataset (Silberer et al., 2020b) into individual instances. The `Target` condition is depicted in which the model was provided with features of the object in the red box; datasets for `Context-Obj` and `Context-Scene` were built in the same way.

objects. An example from the Many Names dataset is shown in the upper part of the Figure 1. In our experiments, we use the dataset splits of ManyNames v2.1 as reported in Silberer et al. (2020b). Specifically, the train / val / test splits consists of 21503 / 1110 / 1072 items respectively.

2.2 Learning scheme

We approach object naming through the prism of referring expression generation. Our objective is to capture human-like variations in naming. Therefore, we shall look into the probability distribution of names that the model produces in a given context. Training a model to approximate naming distribution similar to humans should improve referring expression generation, possibly reducing deterministic nature of the models (van Deemter et al., 2012). However, one problem with the naming distribution in model's output is that it may include invalid or non-human-like naming variations. To address this, we aim for our models to demonstrate shifts in the probability distribution, mirroring the changes observed in human object naming. These shifts are then learned by mapping different representations corresponding to visual context and background knowledge, rather than random noise, with the target names.

While it is possible to build different models per speaker to account for variation among these speakers (Dale and Viethen, 2009), our goal is to develop *a single function* that can approximate such variation across multiple individual describers. We deliberately chose to train such a simple model because it allows us to focus on evaluating the contribution of features to naming variation rather than the model's complexity. We ask if this function can predict the likelihood of a speaker referring to a particular object with a particular name. To answer the question, we break down the individual accumulated counts of frequencies into the number of individual referring events, each consisting of one description. This approach is similar to that of Coventry et al. (2005). The frequency of these events in the dataset reflects the likelihood that the object would be referred to with that name. The bottom part of Figure 1 provides a more detailed example, which involves breaking down the counts of different name types from individual instances. This mirrors how humans describe an image, where each person may use different names for the same object. By learning from these individual instances, the network is expected to learn the variations in naming and, therefore, capture speaker uncertainty. During training, the model is repeatedly presented with input–"car" pair 32 times, while inputs mapped with "vehicle" and "automobile" are shown to the model 2 and 1 time, respectively. This variability in selection is akin to the diverse choices humans make in object naming. By using such training scheme, we encourage the model to learn *uncertainty* inherent in human naming, which is important for capturing variation. In the next section, we will describe how we represent different inputs to the name prediction model.

2.3 Input representation

The dataset consists of the following elements: for the jth sample, there is an image i_j, a target object t_j with a bounding box t_j^{bb} obtained from Visual Genome, and a dictionary V_j containing names and their frequencies assigned to t_j by crowd-workers. Our initial proposal is to use each feature independently as input to a simple classifier to evaluate individual contribution of features. Next, a combination of different features can be explored. In terms of the features, we examine different types of representations which differ in the level of contextual information available. These include features that solely focus on the target object (`Target`), features that incorporate information about surrounding objects but exclude the target object (`Context-Obj`), and features that cover knowledge about the entire scene (`Context-Scene`). For each feature type, we consider three representation modes: visual, linguistic, and their combination. We encode each feature type with CLIP (Radford et al., 2021)[2], a pre-trained multi-modal transformer that learns strong multi-modal representations through its contrastive learning on large amount of image-text pairs. Our motivation for selecting different modalities and combining them is as follows. Text features can be seen as representations of the background knowledge in terms of the meaning of a word in the contexts that were given to the pre-trained model, e.g. CLIP. This knowledge is acquired through extensive pre-training, and CLIP, in particular, possesses rich contextual information about entities and objects. Hence, textual features encode *general* knowledge about the interaction of these objects, not related to particular events (although it is possible that due to naming variation of labels some specific local context is also captured). An example of this type of world knowledge includes the typical contexts in which bananas appear (kitchen, food, nature, market), how they are typically used (eaten, consumed), and who typically uses them (humans, animals). On the other hand, vision features contain information about the immediate context of the target object. Their purpose is to encode the situation in which the object appears in a specific case. Here is an example of this type of feature: a more detailed and specific understanding of the situations in which bananas appear could involve a market with various fruits of different colours and a better understanding of how bananas fit into this specific context. By integrating both these feature types, we take a step toward modelling the information sources that humans employ for object naming. These features include world knowledge about how objects interact in the world and specific visual information about these objects.

In the `Target` condition, our aim is to examine the effect of the knowledge about the target object in the process of object naming. We seek to determine whether a model can effectively capture naming variation in the absence of contextual information, relying solely on the appearance and/or common sense knowledge of the target object. To represent common sense knowledge[3], we use labels that have been assigned to objects (both target and context) by the annotators of the Visual Genome dataset (Krishna et al., 2017). By encoding these labels with CLIP, we can leverage strong signals and extensive additional knowledge about the objects. It is important to note that this type of information is not typically available to a conventional referring expression model. In fact, any identification system that uses this information would be considered cheating in predicting names. In our experiments, we incorporate this knowledge to evaluate its contribution to generating a variety of names, but it is important to acknowledge that this feature may or may not be available in individual tasks.

With the `Context-Obj` condition, we measure how well a target's name can be predicted from surrounding objects alone. In other words, can we "guess" a name based on the visual and/or common sense knowledge about context objects? Finally, with the `Context-Scene` condition, we focus on attention and search: given visual and/or common sense knowledge about the scene as a whole (e.g., all objects treated equally, no difference between context or target objects), can we model human naming variation?

`Target` We represent visual $\mathbf{v}_j^v$ and linguistic $\mathbf{v}_j^\ell$ information about the target object as follows:

$$\mathbf{v}_j^v = f_{\text{CLIP}}\,(t^{\text{bb}}j), \tag{1}$$

$$\mathbf{v}_j^\ell = f_{\text{CLIP}}\,(t_j^{\text{VisGen}}). \tag{2}$$

Here, t_j^{VisGen} represents the label of the target object from Visual Genome.

`Context-Obj` Another type of feature that can be explored is the knowledge of context. In this particular setup, the input representations do not contain any information about the target object, whether visual or common sense-related. This setup can be viewed as a "guessing game" where the model is given a context representation and tasked with predicting the name of an object likely to appear in that context. To model this scenario, we use Visual Genome annotations to represent the context of the target object. Specifically, we extract a list of bounding boxes for all objects that are *not* the target object, denoted as $\mathbf{R}_{\setminus t_j} := (r_1, \ldots, r_K)$, where K is the number of objects in i_j. Then,

$$\bar{\mathbf{v}}_j^v = f_{\text{CLIP}}\,(\mathbf{R}_{\setminus t_j}), \tag{3}$$

$$\bar{\mathbf{v}}_j^\ell = f_{\text{CLIP}}\,(\mathbf{L}_{\setminus t_j}), \tag{4}$$

where $\mathbf{L}_{\setminus t_j}$ is the list of object descriptions, where each element is a simple phrase consisting of a

[2] We use a pre-trained ViT-L/14@336px based on the code from the official CLIP GitHub repository: `https://github.com/openai/CLIP`.

[3] In this study, we use the terms "linguistic" and "common sense" interchangeably, as they both refer to the knowledge and understanding of language-related information and general knowledge about the world.

name and up to five attributes from Visual Genome annotations, e.g. "car black big", and $\bar{\mathbf{v}}$ is the average of the objects or their descriptions. We also apply L2 normalisation on the resulting vector to obtain a more robust context representation. This normalisation helps enhance the discriminative power of all feature vectors and disregards the influence of differences in magnitude and scale[4]. The motivation behind this design choice is further described in Appendix A.

`Context-Scene` In the third experiment, our focus is to examine the predictability of naming variation from the context *as a whole*. We use perceptual features of the entire image that have been encoded with CLIP and incorporate object-relation triplets that describe the content of the scene. These triplets are sourced from the Visual Genome dataset, where each image is annotated with relationships. We note that that these relationships are generated by different crowd-workers, ensuring a diverse range of annotations for our experiment. While the number of relations may differ from image to image, they collectively provide an overview of the objects present in the scene and their associated events. By leveraging these relationships, we can create language input features for the `Context-Scene` model:

$$\mathbf{v_t} = f_{\text{CLIP}}\,(<\text{S}, \text{P}, \text{O}>), \tag{5}$$

where $<\text{S}, \text{P}, \text{O}>$ represents a single string comprising the subject, predicate, and object names of a specific relationship triplet. Since annotated scene contexts in Visual Genome are not predetermined and vary across images, textual descriptions can be constructed in various ways. To generate textual scene descriptions, we shuffle and randomly extract a varied number of relationship strings. We then employ different methods to feed these strings to the CLIP model in order to obtain language features. Subsequently, we evaluate the `Context-Scene` model using each type of text representation to identify the one that demonstrates optimal performance. The selected model is then used in our primary experiments. More details on how the best `Context-Scene` model that uses text was chosen can be found in Appendix B.

[4]In each experiment where we need to create a single vector from a list of vectors, our approach is to first compute the average vector from the list and then normalise it.

3 Model

In this study, we adopt a simple approach by constructing a CLS (classification) model. The objective is to approximate a function that can predict naming variation. The success of this function approximation provides insights into the suitability of the features as predictors of naming variation. The approach is akin to the use of generalised linear models in statistical testing, where we aim to capture the relationships between the features and the predicted labels. To maintain a close connection to linearity, we build a single-layer feed-forward network as our model. We specifically examine the probabilities assigned to all the labels predicted by the model and evaluating their degree of variation against the probabilities assigned by humans.

The model is trained following the scheme outlined in Section 2.2 and takes input representations described in Section 2.3. The model takes $\mathbf{x}$ which is either a concatenation of visual and linguistic features $\mathbf{x} = (\mathbf{v}_v \oplus \mathbf{v}_\ell)$ or a uni-modal feature, e.g. $\mathbf{x} = \mathbf{v}_v$ or $\mathbf{x} = \mathbf{v}_\ell$, where $\mathbf{x} \in \mathbb{R}^{1\times 768}$. The model is trained to predict a target name $\mathbf{y}$ from the set of all possible names that are available: $\mathbf{Y} = \{\mathbf{y}_1, \ldots, \mathbf{y}_N\}$, where $N = 1642$ is the number of all possible names. N is determined by the set of unique names across all data splits. The model is defined as follows:

$$\hat{\mathbf{y}} = \sigma\big(\big(f_2\,(f1\,(\mathbf{x}))\big)\big), \tag{6}$$

where

$$f_1(\mathbf{x}) = \text{ReLU}\,(\text{BN}\,(\mathbf{W}_1\,\mathbf{x} + \mathbf{b_1})\,), \tag{7}$$

$$f_2(\mathbf{x}') = \text{Dropout}\,(\mathbf{W}_w\,\mathbf{x}' + \mathbf{b_2}) \tag{8}$$

where $\mathbf{W}_1 \in \mathbb{R}^{d_1\times d_2}$, and $\mathbf{W}_2 \in \mathbb{R}^{d_2\times 1}$ is output linear layer that produces the list of logits $\tilde{Z} \in \mathbb{R}^{1\times N}$. The model applies $\mathbf{softmax}\ \sigma$ over the last dimension of $\tilde{Z}$ to transform unnormalised scores into name probabilities.We adjust d_1 depending on the type of the experiment: if we test features from a single modality, then $d_1 = 768$, otherwise $d_1 = 1536$. We set $d_2 = 512$ and Dropout $= 0.1$.

All models were trained using a batch size of 64 and standard cross-entropy loss. The Adam optimiser (Kingma and Ba, 2015) with a weight decay of $1e-5$ was used, and the learning rate was set to $4e-3$. During training, the gradients were clipped by their norm per single batch, with a maximum norm set to 3. The models were trained for a total of 200 epochs, and the best model was selected based on the validation loss at the epoch level. Additionally, we used a scheduler, reducing the learning rate if there was no improvement in the loss for three consecutive epochs during validation.

4 Evaluation metrics

To evaluate the general performance of the model, we use multiple metrics. We note that during evaluation, we do not differentiate between top and alternative names. Our model learns that each possible name is valid but to varying degrees based on the frequency of being assigned to an object. The model is never presented with multiple names and their frequencies simultaneously. This means that it does not make comparative judgments about one name being more or less valid than another. Therefore, our results should be interpreted as an assessment of how often the model would use a specific name to describe an object, without considering its relation to other alternatives.

Firstly, we measure the model's ability to predict the top name (e.g., the most frequent name) by looking at accuracy @1. Other degrees of accuracy are also useful to consider, as they indicate whether the top name occurs in the top-*k* predictions generated by the model, where *k* is the number of name types used to describe a specific target in the specific image. The final accuracy scores are reported as averages over the total number of samples. We also compute the mean rank of the ground-truth label among the model's predictions and report the average mean rank (AMR) across all items. Additionally, we measure the perplexity of the models as an indicator of overall predictive performance. Unlike accuracy, which solely focuses on comparing the top name, perplexity allows us to compare the variation in the predictions of different names. However, perplexity does not measure semantic equivalence or similarity between the predicted names and the human-generated names. We note that since we have previously evaluated the success of the model with accuracy, we can assume that such noise is minimised. We compute perplexity $\mathbf{PP}$ by taking the logarithmic base of the entropy and raising it to the power of entropy, e.g. $\mathbf{PP} = \exp^{\mathbf{H}}$.

To evaluate the suitability of features for predicting naming variation, we calculate the entropy (Shannon, 1948) of each model and humans. Entropy helps us quantify uncertainty, and we anticipate that the best model will demonstrate a similar level of uncertainty as humans. To assess the degree of association between the entropy of each model and human responses, we compute Spearman's rank correlation coefficient (Spearman, 1904). This metric measures the monotonic relationship between the two, and it serves as our primary evaluation metric. The way entropy is calculated is slightly different between the model and humans in terms of the probabilities that we use. For the model, we take the degree of belief that the object should be assigned a particular label by the neural network, represented by logits $\tilde{Z}$. These logits are transformed into probabilities using the $\mathbf{softmax}$ function: $\mathbf{P}_m = \sigma(\tilde{Z})$. For humans, we consider the probability (derived from frequencies) that a human would assign a particular label to the object, representing a collective likelihood. For each test item, we collect all available ground-truth human responses (m) and their corresponding frequencies $(x_1, x_2, \ldots, x_m)$. These frequencies are then transformed into probabilities:

$$p_i = \frac{x_i}{\sum_{j=1}^{m} x_j}, \quad \text{for } i = 1, 2, \ldots, m. \tag{9}$$

Next, we construct a new vector $\mathbf{P}_h \in \mathbb{R}^{1 \times N}$, where values in positions corresponding to the positions of each response in the model's dictionary $\mathcal{V}$ (with $|\mathcal{V}| = N$) are replaced with their respective probabilities p_i, and the rest are set to 0. To compute entropy $\mathbf{H}$ of $\mathbf{P}m$ and $\mathbf{P}h$, we use the following operation:

$$\mathbf{H}_{m \backslash h} = - \sum_{k=1}^{|\mathbf{P}_{m \backslash h}|} p_k \log p_k. \tag{10}$$

We normalise the maximum attainable entropy by $-\log \exp(N)$ to ensure comparability between different models, resulting in entropy values ranging between 0 and 1, where 1 represents the highest possible entropy. All metrics are reported as averages across the test set. We anticipate that the model probabilities will show greater variation across labels due to noise compared to humans, as the model may assign low probabilities to labels that are not applicable. On the other hand, humans tend to produce "cleaner" labels as they are direct judgments. To address this issue, we compare the ranks of entropies using correlation coefficients. This choice is relevant because the

	Condition	Mode	Accuracy (%) ↑			AMR ↓	PP ↓	H ↓	ρ
			@1	@5	@10				
1		TEXT	69.15	87.68	89.94	41.45	4.745	0.210	0.540*
2	Target	VISION	56.70	81.09	86.34	52.87	7.199	0.266	0.485*
3		VISION-TEXT	70.02	90.99	92.30	33.77	3.740	0.178	0.574*
4		TEXT	40.90	67.58	76.73	52.13	14.924	0.365	0.343*
5	Context-Obj	VISION	49.14	75.14	83.20	40.79	10.360	0.315	0.328*
6		VISION-TEXT	46.48	72.98	81.04	45.87	11.531	0.330	0.321*
7		TEXT	4.09	16.85	31.80	59.00	51.111	0.531	-0.024
8	Context-Scene	VISION	47.93	73.51	81.42	60.73	9.116	0.298	0.410*
9		VISION-TEXT	53.34	77.91	83.98	38.87	8.281	0.285	0.424*
	Human						**1.623**	**0.065**	**1.000**

Table 1: Evaluation of different features (models 1-9) against human scores. We highlight the top three models **per condition** in each metric, with colour intensity reflecting their performance (stronger indicates better). Human scores are provided as a reference. The values of Spearman correlation ρ with *denote a very high level of significance, e.g. p-value ≤ 0.001.

vector $\mathbf{P}_h$ contains many zero values, which motivates us to focus on the ranks of the values rather than the values themselves. When describing an object, humans select from a limited set of "valid" names, whereas the model considers both "valid" and "invalid" names (a total of 1642 possible name types). By examining the ranks of the model's predictions, we mitigate this issue. We would like to emphasise the general importance of statistical testing to determine the extent to which the model's performance is influenced by either the network design or the features themselves. In this paper, we employ Spearman correlation to measure the relationship between input features and target variables. This test is appropriate because we are interested in whether the simple neural network can approximate a function between input features and the resulting naming variation. This correlation shows whether there is a linear relation between the model's prediction and human scores and, therefore, whether those input features are associated with human scores. We believe that future work can focus on measuring the effects not only of features but also of the model's design on naming variation.

5 Results

Table 1 demonstrates the results of our experiments, which focused on evaluating different feature representations (modes) for various feature types (conditions) in modelling naming variation. Firstly, we examine differences within each condition and analyse different modes to identify the best features for representing specific condition. Next, we explore the differences between conditions and consider the potential of combining them to achieve a more human-like performance in the object identification model. We conclude by emphasising features that need to be encoded by an REG (Referring Expression Generation) model to effectively capture human-like object naming variation.

5.1 Best feature per condition

Representing targets In the Target condition, multi-modality proves to be crucial as it achieves the highest performance in predicting the correct answer, exhibiting the lowest mean rank and perplexity. Additionally, language-and-vision features significantly reduce uncertainty and bring it closer to human levels, as indicated by entropy and correlation measures. Notably, language appears to contribute more to the fusion of modalities, as it offers greater informativeness compared to visual information. This observation aligns with previous studies conducted on various multi-modal tasks (Agrawal et al., 2018). The contribution of the text mode can be attributed to the degree of semantic similarity that an object label from Visual Genome and a target name share with each other. For example, the Visual Genome label for the target object in Figure 1 is "sedan", which is very similar in meaning to the target names, while context labels ("street", "human") might be less useful in reducing uncertainty for naming. Additionally, encoding it with CLIP that is expected to understand relations between "car", "sedan" and "vehicle" might provide even more informative representations, reducing ambiguity about the choice of the name. Nonetheless, the vision representation in the `Target` condition demonstrates good performance, as it does not lag far behind the performance of the text features. One possible explanation for this result is that the knowledge in text is simply not very effective, either due to noise or its challenging nature to learn from, or it may not be very informative. We emphasise that it is important to evaluate the quality of knowledge types in the Limitations section. Interestingly, incorporating visual appearance of the target object further enhances the correlation between the predicted and human naming variation. We conclude that for effectively representing the target object, the most optimal feature representation involves combining visual information with common sense knowledge of the target object.

Representing context as objects In the `Context-Obj` condition, the vision-only model demonstrates the best performance in predicting a single correct name and achieves the lowest mean rank of the correct name in its predictions. It also has the lowest entropy among the different modes considered. However, it is important to note that the vision-only model does not exhibit the highest correlation with human naming variation. The highest correlation is observed when the model relies solely on textual features, despite having the highest entropy among all three modes. This observation is interesting as it emphasises the significance of world knowledge in capturing naming variation. Understanding what objects might co-occur in a given context provides valuable information to the model (Dobnik et al., 2022). For instance, having the context labels "counter", "fridge", and "oven" might assist the model in predicting the target name "pot" more accurately than relying solely on visual features of these context objects. Interestingly, contrary to the `Target` condition, combining linguistic and visual information leads to the lowest correlation score. Based on these results, we conclude that representing context in a model that aims to capture naming variation is best achieved through the textual labels of the context objects.

Representing context as a scene When representing context as a single image with or without relationship triplets, combining language and vision yields the best performance across various metrics, including correlation with humans. There is a notable reduction in uncertainty and an increase in correlation when the model has access to the visual appearance of the context alone, represented by the image as a whole. This improvement can be attributed to the model's ability to better contextualise the target object as text knowledge provides only general information about what context objects are and lacks details on how the objects actually look. In contrast, uncertainty in the model is significantly high when the model is provided with relationship triplets alone. In fact, this condition shows no correlation with human naming at all. The text-only model stands out with exceptionally high perplexity and significantly higher entropy compared to any other model in any of the conditions. We believe this highlights the importance of choosing appropriate representations for conveying textual knowledge about the scene. Exploring the performance of models using other types of representations, such as scene categories, captions, or more coherent scene descriptions, is left as a topic for future investigation. Considering that the task involves mixed representations of targets and context without explicit labelling, the `Context-Scene` model approximates correlation most effectively when there is a fusion of modalities.

Overall, the findings indicate the importance of the text modality in learning about the target object. However, combining text with vision is necessary to achieve lower entropies and higher correlations with human naming. This demonstrates that predicting a name solely from text is challenging because the model lacks knowledge about the appearance of objects and struggles to determine what to focus on. Access to visual representations allows the model to differentiate between targets and contexts, possibly due to factors such as the perspective and location of the objects, which are relevant for naming. In the next section, we focus on identifying the optimal feature combination for better object naming. Our goal is to assess the correlation with human naming when multiple conditions are combined, thereby determining the best possible combination of features.

Condition	Accuracy (%) ↑			AMR ↓	PP ↓	H ↓	ρ
	@1	@5	@10				
3+9	71.02	88.59	90.62	**37.66**	**3.773**	**0.179**	**0.580***
3+4	70.55	88.76	90.62	43.02	4.187	0.193	0.568*
3+9+4	**71.41**	**89.73**	**91.42**	38.96	3.995	0.187	0.578*

Table 2: Evaluation of different combinations of the best-performing features from Table 1. The meaning of colour intensity and *is described in Table 1. The numbers in condition correspond to the features from Table 1.

5.2 Combining best-performing features

Here we test different feature combinations to replicate human-like naming variation. We acknowledge that without testing of *all* possible combinations, we cannot really conclude which feature combination is the best. However, here we have chosen feature combinations based on our intuition regarding what is commonly found in models and what yields the best performance when considering individual features. Table 2 presents the results of combining features that have shown the highest correlation with humans across different conditions. For each condition, we progressively combined features that showed the highest correlation with humans by concatenating them together. As a result, the input vector size for the 3+9+4 condition became 5×768, representing the combination of two modalities for the target, two modalities for the context as a scene, and one modality for the context as objects. The best model, which incorporates visual and common sense knowledge about the target (3 in Table 1) along with multi-modal knowledge about the scene (9 in Table 1), achieves the lowest entropy and improves the correlation with humans compared to the previously best model, the `Target` model. This indicates that combining the appearance of an object, including its label, with the shared context and thematic representation of the scene as a whole can be beneficial. Interestingly, combining different features with each other generally yields better results than using them individually, except for the combination of the best `Target` and `Context-Obj` models. The optimal combination is found to be the integration of knowledge about the target with knowledge about the scene as a whole. Notably, the 3+9 combination achieves lower accuracies, suggesting that it may be more focused on capturing variation rather than predicting the most probable name. These findings have implications for the representation of context. While the visual appearance of objects is important, it also needs to be presented in a consistent and comprehensive manner, such as using a whole image where the relationships among context objects are clear, and the fit of the target within the overall context can be easily extracted.

6 Conclusions

Naming and language in general is semantically underspecified (Frisson, 2009; Pezzelle, 2023). To fill in the missing gaps in reconstructing meaning, language users rely on contextual information, be it perceptual information or background knowledge. In this study we examined different types of context representations for capturing human object naming variation. We have found that to capture naming variation it is important to have a lot of knowledge about the target object. We also have shown that the way context is represented matters: object-level visual representations might narrow down the gap in uncertainty between models and humans, but they might not correlate the most with humans in object naming. Future work on this topic should focus on using encoders other than CLIP, building more complex classifiers and investigating the effect of different ways to represent common sense knowledge (e.g., not relationship triplets, but captions or another type of image descriptions). Also, looking at object naming in a task context with communicative goal is another important direction.

Limitations

Information fusion This work uses averaging to generate a single vector when combining multiple language and/or vision features. It should be acknowledged that adopting an alternative fusion method, such as multiplication or summation, could potentially affect the final scores of the models, particularly when the differences between them are relatively minor. We recognise that the results reported in this study are specific to the particular technical setup employed, involving L2 normalisation with averaging. Hence, further investigation is warranted to determine whether the reported findings remain consistent when using a different fusion method. Some of our ideas for information fusion are presented in Appendix A. In addition, fusing different features from different conditions by multiplying them or learning a function to fuse them can be an alternative to a simple concatenation that we use in this study.

Knowledge representations We note that in the context of a standard REG task, knowing the label of the target is practically impossible. Hence, it is expected that a model with linguistic knowledge about the target would perform well. Also, adding more features (visual, linguistic, others) appears to hinder performance due to the increased number of parameters and a larger hypothesis space. Therefore, the objective of learning should be to strike a balance between model size and feature informativeness. It is also important to seek a knowledge representation that closely resembles how humans name objects.

Acknowledgments

The research in this paper is supported by a grant from the Swedish Research Council (VR project 2014-39) for the establishment of the Centre for Linguistic Theory and Studies in Probability (CLASP) at the University of Gothenburg.

References

Aishwarya Agrawal, Dhruv Batra, Devi Parikh, and Aniruddha Kembhavi. 2018. Don't just assume; look and answer: Overcoming priors for visual question answering. In *2018 IEEE Conference on Computer Vision and Pattern Recognition, CVPR 2018, Salt Lake City, UT, USA, June 18-22, 2018*, pages 4971–4980. Computer Vision Foundation / IEEE Computer Society.

Malihe Alikhani and Matthew Stone. 2019. "Caption" as a coherence relation: Evidence and implications. In *Proceedings of the Second Workshop on Shortcomings in Vision and Language*, pages 58–67, Minneapolis, Minnesota. Association for Computational Linguistics.

Jacob Andreas. 2022. Language models as agent models. In *Findings of the Association for Computational Linguistics: EMNLP 2022*, pages 5769–5779, Abu Dhabi, United Arab Emirates. Association for Computational Linguistics.

Adriana Baltaretu, Emiel Krahmer, and Alfons Maes. 2019. Producing referring expressions in identification tasks and route directions: What's the difference? *Discourse Processes*, 56(2):136–154.

S.E. Brennan and H.H. Clark. 1996. Conceptual Pacts and Lexical Choice in Conversation. *Learning, Memory*, 22(6):1482–1493.

K.R. Coventry, A. Cangelosi, R. Rajapakse, A. Bacon, S. Newstead, D. Joyce, and L.V. Richards. 2005. Spatial prepositions and vague quantifiers:: Implementing the functional geometric framework. In *Spatial Cognition IV.*, volume IV, pages 98–110, United States. Springer Nature. Error 1 : ISSN or ISBN parsed from 0302-9743 but is invalid for outputType A which is a Book.

Robert Dale and Jette Viethen. 2009. Referring expression generation through attribute-based heuristics. In *Proceedings of the 12th European Workshop on Natural Language Generation (ENLG 2009)*, pages 58–65, Athens, Greece. Association for Computational Linguistics.

Simon Dobnik, Nikolai Ilinykh, and Aram Karimi. 2022. What to refer to and when? reference and re-reference in two language-and-vision tasks. In *Proceedings of the 26th Workshop on the Semantics and Pragmatics of Dialogue - Full Papers*, Dublin, Ireland. SEMDIAL.

Michael C. Frank and Noah D. Goodman. 2012. Predicting pragmatic reasoning in language games. *Science*, 336(6084):998–998.

Daniel Fried, Nicholas Tomlin, Jennifer Hu, Roma Patel, and Aida Nematzadeh. 2023. Pragmatics in language grounding: Phenomena, tasks, and modeling approaches.

Steven Frisson. 2009. Semantic underspecification in language processing. *Lang. Linguistics Compass*, 3(1):111–127.

Mario Giulianelli. 2022. Towards pragmatic production strategies for natural language generation tasks. In *Proceedings of the 2022 Conference on Empirical Methods in Natural Language Processing*, pages 7978–7984, Abu Dhabi, United Arab Emirates. Association for Computational Linguistics.

Caroline Graf, Judith Degen, Robert X. D. Hawkins, and Noah D. Goodman. 2016. Animal, dog, or dalmatian? level of abstraction in nominal referring expressions. In *Proceedings of the 38th Annual Meeting of the Cognitive Science Society, Recogbizing and Representing Events, CogSci 2016, Philadelphia, PA, USA, August 10-13, 2016*. cognitivesciencesociety.org.

Eleonora Gualdoni, Thomas Brochhagen, Andreas Mädebach, and Gemma Boleda. 2022a. What's in a name? a large-scale computational study on how competition between names affects naming variation.

Eleonora Gualdoni, Thomas Brochhagen, Andreas Mädebach, and Gemma Boleda. 2022b. Woman or tennis player? visual typicality and lexical frequency affect variation in object naming.

Eleonora Gualdoni, Andreas Madebach, Thomas Brochhagen, and Gemma Boleda. 2022c. Horse or pony? Visual typicality and lexical frequency affect variability in object naming. In *Proceedings of the Society for Computation in Linguistics 2022*, pages 241–243, online. Association for Computational Linguistics.

Nikolai Ilinykh, Sina Zarrieß, and David Schlangen. 2018. The task matters: Comparing image captioning and task-based dialogical image description. In *Proceedings of the 11th International Conference on Natural Language Generation*, pages 397–402, Tilburg University, The Netherlands. Association for Computational Linguistics.

Sahar Kazemzadeh, Vicente Ordonez, Mark Matten, and Tamara Berg. 2014. ReferItGame: Referring to objects in photographs of natural scenes. In *Proceedings of the 2014 Conference on Empirical Methods in Natural Language Processing (EMNLP)*, pages 787–798, Doha, Qatar. Association for Computational Linguistics.

Diederik P. Kingma and Jimmy Ba. 2015. Adam: A method for stochastic optimization. In *ICLR (Poster)*.

Emiel Krahmer and Kees van Deemter. 2012. Computational generation of referring expressions: A survey. *Computational Linguistics*, 38(1):173–218.

Elisa Kreiss, Cynthia Bennett, Shayan Hooshmand, Eric Zelikman, Meredith Ringel Morris, and Christopher Potts. 2022. Context matters for image descriptions for accessibility: Challenges for referenceless evaluation metrics. In *Proceedings of the 2022 Conference on Empirical Methods in Natural Language Processing*, pages 4685–4697, Abu Dhabi, United Arab Emirates. Association for Computational Linguistics.

Ranjay Krishna, Yuke Zhu, Oliver Groth, Justin Johnson, Kenji Hata, Joshua Kravitz, Stephanie Chen, Yannis Kalantidis, Li-Jia Li, David A. Shamma, Michael S. Bernstein, and Li Fei-Fei. 2017. Visual genome: Connecting language and vision using crowdsourced dense image annotations. *Int. J. Comput. Vis.*, 123(1):32–73.

Tsung-Yi Lin, Michael Maire, Serge J. Belongie, James Hays, Pietro Perona, Deva Ramanan, Piotr Dollár, and C. Lawrence Zitnick. 2014. Microsoft COCO: common objects in context. In *Computer Vision - ECCV 2014 - 13th European Conference, Zurich, Switzerland, September 6-12, 2014, Proceedings, Part V*, volume 8693 of *Lecture Notes in Computer Science*, pages 740–755. Springer.

Margaret Mitchell, Ehud Reiter, and Kees van Deemter. 2013. Typicality and object reference. *Cognitive Science*, 35:3062–3067.

Andreas Mädebach, Ekaterina Torubarova, Eleonora Gualdoni, and Gemma Boleda. 2022. Effects of task and visual context on referring expressions using natural scenes.

Sandro Pezzelle. 2023. Dealing with semantic underspecification in multimodal NLP. In *Proceedings of the 61st Annual Meeting of the Association for Computational Linguistics (Volume 1: Long Papers)*, pages 12098–12112, Toronto, Canada. Association for Computational Linguistics.

Bryan A. Plummer, Liwei Wang, Chris M. Cervantes, Juan C. Caicedo, Julia Hockenmaier, and Svetlana Lazebnik. 2015. Flickr30k entities: Collecting region-to-phrase correspondences for richer image-to-sentence models. In *2015 IEEE International Conference on Computer Vision, ICCV 2015, Santiago, Chile, December 7-13, 2015*, pages 2641–2649. IEEE Computer Society.

Alec Radford, Jong Wook Kim, Chris Hallacy, Aditya Ramesh, Gabriel Goh, Sandhini Agarwal, Girish Sastry, Amanda Askell, Pamela Mishkin, Jack Clark, Gretchen Krueger, and Ilya Sutskever. 2021. Learning transferable visual models from natural language supervision. In *Proceedings of the 38th International Conference on Machine Learning, ICML 2021, 18-24 July 2021, Virtual Event*, volume 139 of *Proceedings of Machine Learning Research*, pages 8748–8763. PMLR.

Ehud Reiter and Robert Dale. 2000. *Building Natural Language Generation Systems*. Natural Language Processing. Cambridge University Press.

David Schlangen. 2022. Norm participation grounds language. In *Proceedings of the 2022 CLASP Conference on (Dis)embodiment*, pages 62–69, Gothenburg, Sweden. Association for Computational Linguistics.

Simeon Schüz, Albert Gatt, and Sina Zarrieß. 2023. Rethinking symbolic and visual context in referring expression generation. *Frontiers in Artificial Intelligence*, 6.

C. E. Shannon. 1948. A mathematical theory of communication. *Bell System Technical Journal*, 27(3):379–423.

Carina Silberer, Sina Zarrieß, and Gemma Boleda. 2020a. Object naming in language and vision: A survey and a new dataset. In *Proceedings of The 12th Language Resources and Evaluation Conference*, pages 5792–5801, Marseille, France. European Language Resources Association.

Carina Silberer, Sina Zarrieß, Matthijs Westera, and Gemma Boleda. 2020b. Humans meet models on object naming: A new dataset and analysis. In *Proceedings of the 28th International Conference on Computational Linguistics*, pages 1893–1905, Barcelona, Spain (Online). International Committee on Computational Linguistics.

Charles Spearman. 1904. The proof and measurement of association between two things. *The American Journal of Psychology*, 15(1):72–101.

Robert Stalnaker. 1978. Assertion. *Syntax and Semantics (New York Academic Press)*, 9:315–332.

Kees van Deemter, Albert Gatt, Roger P.G. van Gompel, and Emiel Krahmer. 2012. Toward a computational psycholinguistics of reference production. *Topics in Cognitive Science*, 4(2):166–183.

Kees van Deemter, Ielka van der Sluis, and Albert Gatt. 2006. Building a semantically transparent corpus for the generation of referring expressions. In *Proceedings of the Fourth International Natural Language Generation Conference*, pages 130–132, Sydney, Australia. Association for Computational Linguistics.

Emiel van Miltenburg. 2017. Pragmatic descriptions of perceptual stimuli. In *Proceedings of the Student Research Workshop at the 15th Conference of the European Chapter of the Association for Computational Linguistics*, pages 1–10, Valencia, Spain. Association for Computational Linguistics.

Licheng Yu, Patrick Poirson, Shan Yang, Alexander C. Berg, and Tamara L. Berg. 2016. Modeling context in referring expressions. In *Computer Vision - ECCV 2016 - 14th European Conference, Amsterdam, The Netherlands, October 11-14, 2016, Proceedings, Part II*, volume 9906 of *Lecture Notes in Computer Science*, pages 69–85. Springer.

A Fusing features

In our approach, when it is necessary to combine multiple uni-modal or multi-modal representations into a single vector, we use averaging of features. This averaging process is followed by an L2 normalisation step, which normalises the features based on the Euclidean distance between individual points. Additionally, we have experimented with using multiplication for feature fusion, particularly in cases where we want to emphasise joint features or attributes and assign more importance to overlapping information. Multiplication is expected to highlight specific features that are shared across objects, such as in the case of visual features. However, we have observed that multiplication often leads to many zero values in the resulting features, and in some cases, it even leads to inf or NaN values due to the sparsity of visual representations. This sparsity can make the resulting vector difficult to learn from, especially depending on the number of objects being multiplied. Although summation of features is a straightforward approach, we have concerns that using this method results in a diluted final vector. As a result, we decided to use averaging followed by L2 normalisation as it tends to be a more effective and stable approach for feature combination.

B Representing language for `Context-Scene`

Table 3 presents the performance of various variations of the `Context-Scene` model, which incorporates the textual modality. The text representation can be either a single string containing 10 or 5 relations present in the image (`10-string` and `5-string`), or a list of different relations (`10-list` and `5-list`). The best model is selected based on the loss and average mean rank score, both computed on the test set. The best-performing model is highlighted in bold in the table.

Condition	Text Format	Accuracy (%) ↑			AMR ↓	Loss ↓
		@1	@5	@10		
Context-Scene + Text	10-list	4.04	17.98	30.43	62.63	4.774
	10-string	4.09	16.85	31.80	**59.00**	**4.676**
	5-list	3.83	16.69	31.70	63.32	4.756
	5-string	3.58	16.99	30.80	125.50	5.722
Context-Scene + Vision-Text	10-list	52.40	75.58	83.09	45.49	2.490
	10-string	53.27	77.27	83.24	43.38	2.463
	5-list	52.44	76.68	83.11	45.12	2.475
	5-string	53.34	77.91	83.98	**38.87**	**2.403**

Table 3: Performance of different Context-Scene models, which use textual modality as part of their input.

The Scenario Refin*er*: Grounding subjects in images at the morphological level

Tagliaferri Claudia
Utrecht University
cl.tagliaferri@outlook.com

Axioti Sofia
Leiden University
s.axioti@outlook.com

Gatt Albert
Utrecht University
a.gatt@uu.nl

Paperno Denis
Utrecht University
d.paperno@uu.nl

Abstract

Derivationally related words, such as "runner" and "running", exhibit semantic differences which also elicit different visual scenarios. In this paper, we ask whether Vision and Language (V&L) models capture such distinctions at the morphological level, using a a new methodology and dataset. We compare the results from V&L models to human judgements and find that models' predictions differ from those of human participants, in particular displaying a grammatical bias. We further investigate whether the human-model misalignment is related to model architecture. Our methodology, developed on one specific morphological contrast, can be further extended for testing models on capturing other nuanced language features.

1 Introduction

Vision and language (V&L) models are trained to ground linguistic descriptions in visual data. These models differ in pre-training and architecture. In particular, there are differences in the cross-modal information exchange between the textual and visual streams of the models (Frank et al., 2021; Parcalabescu and Frank, 2022), even though sometimes, as shown for V&L models based on the BERT architecture (Devlin et al., 2019), architectural differences have little impact on downstream performance for many benchmarks (Bugliarello et al., 2021).

Pre-trained V&L models achieve high performance on diverse benchmarks, such as question answering, image retrieval and word masking (Tan and Bansal, 2019). However, they have limitations in tasks requiring *fine-grained* understanding (Bugliarello et al., 2023), including the ability to reason compositionally in visually grounded settings (Thrush et al., 2022), distinguish spatial relationships and quantities (Parcalabescu et al., 2020, 2022), and identify dependencies between verbs and arguments (Hendricks and Nematzadeh, 2021). Most of these fine-grained linguistic phenomena are at the interface between syntax and semantics.

Far less attention has been paid to grounding fine-grained linguistic features at the morphological level. We aim to address this gap by investigating multimodal alignment at the morphological level. We focus on derived nouns with the agentive suffix *-er* (e.g. *baker*) and the corresponding verbal form (*baking*). Such derivationally related pairs involve both category-level and semantic contrasts, with corresponding differences in the typical visual scenarios they evoke. For instance, human judges would accept the description *x is baking* for a variety of visual scenes depicting a person (hereafter referred to as 'the subject') performing a particular action. Only a subset of such images would, however, also be judged as corresponding to *x is a baker*, since the agentive noun introduces additional expectations, for example about the way the subject is dressed or the physical environment they are in. By analysing the same stem (e.g. *bake*) in different parts of speech, we explore the ability of V&L models to capture the subtle differences in meaning and visual representation. To do this, we rely on a zero-shot setting in which we test the probability with which pretrained V&L models match an image to a corresponding text containing an agentive noun or a verb, comparing this to human judgments about the same image-text pairs.

Our contributions are: (i) a methodology for testing V&L models on morphological contrasts; (ii) a dataset of images that highlights the contrast between verbs and derived nouns, annotated with human judgements; (iii) an analysis of the V&L models' predictions on the contrast between derivationally related verbs and nouns, in comparison to human judgements.

Proceedings of the 1st Workshop on Linguistic Insights from and for Multimodal Language Processing, pages 25–33
September 22, 2023.

2 Related work

2.1 Models

Various V&L model architectures have been proposed, differing a.o. in the way visual vs. textual features are processed. One important distinction, common among models based on the BERT architecture, is between single- and dual-stream models. The former concatenate inputs in the two modalities and process them through a common transformer stack; the latter first process each modality through its own transformer stack, before performing cross-modal attention at a later stage (Bugliarello et al., 2021). Another influential architecture is the dual encoder (Radford et al., 2021), which is trained to project visual and textual embeddings into a common multimodal space. Among their pretraining objectives, BERT-based V&L models typically include *image-text matching*, whereby the model returns a probability that an image corresponds with a caption. Thus, such models can be tested zero-shot on image-text pairs. For dual encoders, similar insights can be obtained by comparing the distance in multimodal space between a text and an image embedding.

We aim to understand the impact of these architectures on the morphological contrast between word categories and whether the classification depends on specific visual information. Three models with different architectures and pre-training phases are tested: CLIP (Radford et al., 2021), ViLT (Kim et al., 2021), and LXMERT (Tan and Bansal, 2019).

CLIP employs a *dual encoder* architecture and projects image and text embeddings in a common space, such that corresponding image-text pairs are closer than non-corresponding ones. CLIP is pre-trained using cross-modal contrastive learning on internet-sourced image-text pairs, resulting in strong multimodal representations (Radford et al., 2021). Two different visual backbones are used for the image encoder: ResNet50 (He et al., 2016), which uses attention pooling; and the Vision Transformer (Dosovitskiy et al., 2020) which is modified by the addition of an additional layer normalisation to the combined patch and position embedding. The text encoder is a Transformer which operates on a lower-cased byte pair encoding (BPE) representation of the text. CLIP computes the cosine similarity between an image and a text.

LXMERT follows a *dual-stream* approach, utilising three encoders: an object relationship encoder which acts upon the output of a faster-RCNN visual backbone (Ren et al., 2015), a language encoder, and a cross-modality transformer stack which applies attention across the two modalities. The pretraining involves five tasks, including masked cross-modality language modelling and image question answering, enabling the model to establish intra-modality and cross-modality relationships (Tan and Bansal, 2019). LXMERT is also pretrained with an image-text alignment head, which computes the probability that a text and an image correspond.

ViLT (Kim et al., 2021) is the simplest V&L architecture used in this study. It is a single-stream model in which a single transformer stack processes the concatenation of visual and textual features. In contrast to other models, no pre-trained visual backbone is used; rather, the model works directly on pixel-level inputs, in the spirit of Dosovitskiy et al. (2020). It has been shown that the usage of word masking and image augmentations improves its performance (Kim et al., 2021). In ViLT, the embedding layers of raw pixels and text tokens are shallow and computationally light. This architecture thereby concentrates most of the computation on modelling modality interactions. Like LXMERT, ViLT is also pre-trained with an image-text alignment head, in addition to the multimodal masked modelling objective.

2.2 Related studies

Our work is related to studies focusing on the *typicality* of the word-image relationship and the interplay with category labels for images depicting people. For example, people can be described using generic expressions referring to gender or more specific expressions highlighting individual properties or aspects. Visual properties that align with our conceptual knowledge of the noun may lead us to prefer agentive expressions over generic nouns such as "man" or "woman" (Corbetta, 2021). Gualdoni et al. (2022a,b) proposed ManyNames, a small dataset that explores the factors that affect naming variation for visual objects, for instance, the different conceptualisations of the same object (e.g., "woman" vs. "tennis player") or the disambiguation of the nature of the object (e.g., "horse" vs. "pony"). Understanding the effects of context and naming preferences is crucial for V&L models to gain comprehensive understanding of visual scenes. The *typicality of the context* determines the occurrence of specific names based on the global scene

Noun	Verb	Noun	Verb
supporter	supporting	lover	loving
baker	baking	surfer	surfing
runner	running	swimmer	swimming
hunter	hunting	driver	driving
painter	painting	skier	skiing
walker	walking	dancer	dancing
singer	singing	gamer	gaming
teacher	teaching	reader	reading
cleaner	cleaning	smoker	smoking

Table 1: Noun-verb pairs in the Scenario Refin*er* dataset

(a)

Annotation 1: The man and the woman are supporters
Annotation 2: The man and the woman are supporting

Annotation 1: The woman with pink gloves is a driver
Annotation 2: The woman with pink gloves is driving

Figure 1: Sample of stimuli for *supporter-supporting* and *driver-driving*

where the subject is situated.

The current study explores the impact of typicality of the context at the morphological level. Derivational relations, relating two words or whole paradigms of words (Bonami and Strnadová, 2019), involve contrasts at different levels, including form, syntax – where the words are related but belong to different word categories – and semantics, where the meaning of one member contrasts with the meanings of the other members. For instance, *runner* and *run* belong to the same paradigm, but the suffix *-er* changes the word category and alters the referential meaning of the verb. For example, "the man is a runner" evokes a fit person who frequently trains, while "the man is running" could equally well portray a man casually running to catch a train. Thus, derived noun subjects should embody characteristics of the verb and/or common knowledge. Therefore, syntactic and relational knowledge has to be integrated with semantic knowledge, common imaginary and visual information, as has been argued from the language acquisition perspective (Tyler and Nagy, 1989).

3 Methodology

3.1 Dataset

We create the Scenario Refin*er* dataset highlighting the cognitive and semantic differences between the verb and its derived noun by contrasting one image with two annotations. The dataset is based on 18 word pairs, each consisting of a verb in the *-ing* form and a derived agentive (*-er*) noun. The pairs are summarised in Table 1. The lexical pairs are classified into four conceptual domains: the professional domain (like *baker* or *teacher*), the sports domain (like *runner* or *skier*), the artistic domain (like *dancer* or *painter*), and general (*lover* or *smoker*).

Six images were selected for each of the 18 word pairs. These were manually selected from various sources: Visual Genome (Krishna et al., 2017), Wikipedia Commons, MSCOCO (Lin et al., 2014) and Geograph (`https://www.geograph.org.uk/`).

For the 18 word pairs, we want to compare images which correspond to the stereotypical representation of the agent role described by the derived noun, versus the more general scenario described by the verb. In order to depict the subject denoted by a derived noun, the images need to include additional information compared to the verb, for example, specific objects like tools or outfits for *painter* or *surfer*; or a specific environment like a stage for *dancer* or *singer*. The verbs correspond to a more general scenario, which creates a linguistic and visual contrast with the scenario evoked by the derived noun. This allows us to examine the contrast in parts of speech and their typicality within the defined global scene (Gualdoni et al., 2022b).

For each word pair, 6 images were selected. Each image is accompanied by two captions, as shown in Figure 1. Each caption received a judgement on a Likert scale.

3.2 Data collection

We implemented a survey on Qualtrics and distributed it on Prolific. The survey included 162 images, consisting of 54 fillers and (18 × 6 =) 108 target images representing the 18 selected lexical pairs.

Our survey also included fillers of several types. In one type, images were accompanied by a verb-based description and a derived noun in *-er*, enhanced by an adjective based on the mood or facial expression of the depicted subjects. For instance, a smiling subject wearing appropriate outfit on a ski slope was paired with the captions "The man is a *happy skier*" and "The man *is skiing*". This type of filler aimed to investigate if participants would alter their evaluation when the mental representation of the derived noun is reinforced by additional linguistic information. Another type of filler contrasted the verb and its derived adjective in *-ive*, offering insights into the classification of other members in the morphological paradigm. For example, four men intensely engaged in a video game were paired with the sentences "The men are *competitive*" and "The men *are competing*". A third type of filler contrasted verbs to bare adjectives, descriptive or emotional, to determine participants' preference between verbal and adjectival descriptions. For instance, a couple swimming happily in a lake was matched with "The man and woman are happy" and "The man and woman are swimming"; an image of a man speaking in a classroom was paired with "The man is upright" and "The man is teaching". The fourth type of filler included images with true and false descriptions of the visual content, used to maintain participants' attention and allowing to control the quality of their responses.

For each image, participants were asked to what extent both captions describe the visual scenario, using a seven-point Likert scale ranging from *totally disagree* to *totally agree*. By asking to evaluate both captions for each picture, it is possible to extract a reliable measure of contrast between the derived noun and the verb.

In order not to risk rough human evaluations and minimise participant dropout rates due to the length of the survey, the target images were divided equally between two surveys (each with a total of 81 images where 54 were target images and 27 fillers).

Twenty native British English speakers completed the online questionnaire and were randomly assigned to one of the two surveys. Thus, each image is evaluated by 10 participants for both captions. For the instructions see Appendix A

4 Results

Our analysis proceeds in two stages. We first consider the *category preference*: for an image with two captions (one with a derived noun and one with a verb), we ask whether human judges (resp. V&L models) exhibit a preference for the noun or the verb with respect to a given image. We then compute correlations between the preferences exhibited by human judges and by models for the two categories.

4.1 The word category preference

To analyse which of the two captions is preferred for each image by human judges, we compare the average ratings of the annotations. For V&L models, we consider the difference in probability estimated by a model's image-text matching head (in the case of ViLT and LXMERT) for the caption containing the noun or verb, or the difference in cosine distance between image and caption embeddings (in the case of CLIP). Note that we include results for three versions of CLIP, with different visual backbones. We use a Fisher test to determine whether there is a significant difference in category preference between human judges and V&L models.

Table 2 displays the proportion of times the derived noun or the verb was preferred by humans and by each of the models.

Human judgments Overall, human judges exhibit a preference for captions containing the verb, with only a small percentage of preferences for captions containing agent nominals. These types of classifications are distributed across different domains. This could be due to variation in the images in the extent to which they gave clear visual cues as to the role of the person depicted. There were some exceptions to this trend. In the sports domain, these included images of a skier wearing skiing gear with a cape, and a couple of surfers in surfing attire with surfboards. In the profession domain, they included two images depicting individuals engaged in driving and one image of teachers with pupils posing for a class photo. Four agent nominals belonged to the artistic and general domains, such as images of women dancing on a stage, two subjects getting cigarettes, and a woman in a bookshop. On the other hand, the difference in preference some noun-verb pairs was lower than for others (with differences in the 0–0.5 range). An example is shown in Figure 2, where participants interpreted both

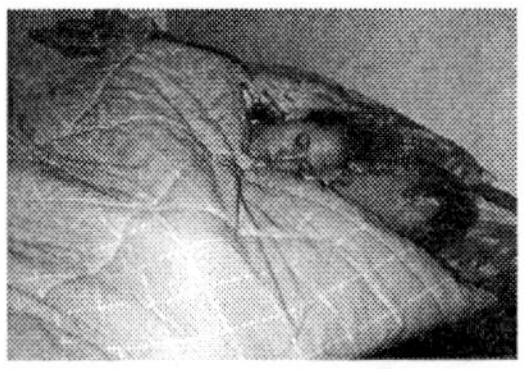

(a) M = 5.50 (noun, verb), SD = 1.20 (noun, verb)

(b) M = 6.30 (noun, verb), SD = 0.90 (noun, verb)

(c) M = 5.30 (noun, verb), SD = 0.90 (noun), 1.00 (verb)

Figure 2: Mean (M) human judgments and standard deviations (SD) for an example image set corresponding to *lover-loving*.

captions as appropriate. Interestingly, the versions of CLIP and LXMERT seem to agree with the human ratings in this example, showing low contrast between the verb and the noun, with LXMERT assigning higher probability to verb caption for (c) and CLIP estimating lower distance between image and verb caption for (a). On the other hand, ViLT assigned a higher probability to the verbal caption for all the images in Figure 2.

V&L models Unlike participants, V&L models exhibit a **tendency to prefer deverbal nouns to verbs**. The exceptions are CLIP with the ViT-B/32 backbone, and ViLT, both of which have a slightly higher preference for captions with verbs. The performance of CLIP seems to depend on the visual backbone. Of the three versions, ViT-L/14 displays the greatest similarity to human judgments. We observed a tendency for ViT-B/32 to prefer captions with derived nouns where there are clear visual cues suggesting a role or activity, such as the microphone and the stage in Figure 3. In contrast, while CLIP-RN50 prefers the noun caption in Figure 3(a), it shows the opposite trend, in favour of

(a) noun: M = 6.20, SD = 1.17; verb: M = 6.50, SD = 1.02

(b) noun: M = 6.20, SD = 1.17; verb: M = 6.50, SD = 1.02

Figure 3: Mean (M) human judgments and standard deviations (SD) for an example image set corresponding to *singer-singing*

	Derived noun	Verb
Humans	8.3%	91.7%
CLIP ViT-L/14@336px	51.9%	48.1%
CLIP RN50x64	52.8%	47.2%
CLIP ViT-B/32	49.1%	50.9%
ViLT	47.2%	52.8%
LXMERT	51.9%	48.1%

Table 2: Preference for derived noun vs. verb, in human judgments and V&L model image-text alignment.

the verb-based caption, in (b), perhaps because the stage is less clearly visible.

The difference between the judgements of humans vs. V&L models is statistically significant (Fisher's exact test, $p < 0.001$ for all contrasts between models and human judgments).

4.2 Correlations between judgements

We also estimate the correlation between human and automatic judgements as a more fine-grained measure than binary preference. Overall, the correlation between the human and the automatic judgements varies depending on architecture and on the conceptual domain.

We assess correlations between three kinds of values: the (human- or model-produced) scores for a) noun and b) verb-based captions, as well as c) the difference between the noun and verb scores. We refer to the latter as the *morphological contrast*.

Participant consistency To assess the consistency of collected human judgements, we split participants randomly into two equal-sized samples and calculate Pearson correlation coefficients between the average scores of the two samples. The resulting correlation coefficients for all conceptual domains are reported in Table 3. Correlation coefficients for noun, verb and contrast are generally consistent, with the exception of the artistic domain, for which correlations between judgments for verb-based captions, and as a consequence, also for the contrast, exhibit more variation.

Models vs human judgments Table 4 displays the overall correlations between human judgments and model image-text alignment for verbs, nouns and the morphological contrast. The correlations are moderate-to-weak, suggesting a lack of alignment between human intuitions and V&L models. This is consistent with our earlier observation that models tend to exhibit different preferences for nouns versus verbs, compared to humans. Interestingly, ViLT emerges as the most correlated model with human judgement in the verbal evaluation, but it exhibits the least correlation in the evaluation of the derived noun. Additionally, ViLT displays a moderate positive relationship with the contrast between verb and derived noun, whereas the other models demonstrate weaker positive correlations or very weak negative correlations with this particular contrast.

Table 5 breaks down correlations by conceptual domain. In the professional domain, correlations are generally stronger, especially for ViLT, LXMERT and CLIP ViT-B/32. Overall, it appears that models correlate with human judges in some domains more than others. Nevertheless, correlations are often negative, and these results suggest a qualitative difference between the image-text alignment performed by models, and the types of knowledge and inferences that humans bring to bear to support the grounding of nominal agentive versus verbal forms in visual stimuli.

5 Discussion

The findings revealed a discrepancy between models and human judgments. Humans displayed a preference for captions containing verbs, whereas V&L models exhibited a preference for nominal descriptions. Participants prefer the derived noun only for a few instances that had additional characteristics elicited by visual elements, or by the kind of action performed by the human subjects in the images. For instance, they prefer the derived noun for two images showing a person getting or purchasing cigarettes (*smoker-smoking*), meaning that participants interpreted the *intention* as a characteristic that corresponds to the derived noun. In contrast, the tested models appeared to prioritise more the action itself rather than the individual who performs the action.

However, examining certain lexical pairs, we observed a greater variance in the pattern of interpretation, highlighting the difficulty in defining the human evaluation of the derived noun. For example, in the sport domain, participants rarely seem to rely on the outfit worn by the subject to base their interpretation, with the exception of *skier*, which happened to be paired only with an image of a subject also exhibiting their competition number. As a surprising contrast, two pictures for *runner-running* similarly depicted subjects with their competition numbers are not evaluated as such by participants. Specifically, one image depicts a man running in a race track, while the other image depicts three men wearing specific outfits running in the countryside. The contrast between the means of the human evaluation is less than or equal to 0.50, indicating the preference for the verbal description.

The models, too, exhibit variety in the subject classification for these images. For example, while CLIP-ViT-L/14@336p, CLIP-ViT-B/32 and ViLT display a similar preference for the nominal form, as humans do, for *skier-skiing*, CLIP-RN50x64 and LXMERT prefer the verb-based caption. Similarly, while participants slightly prefer the verb for the subjects wearing a competition number for *runner-running*, models prefer the nominal description. The three versions of CLIP strongly prefer the derived noun for these subjects, ViLT prefers the verbal description only for the single subject running in a race track and LXMERT prefers the verbal description only for the three subjects running in the countryside. While CLIP exhibited a preference for the derived noun in presence of additional visual elements, ViLT and LXMERT do not seem to base their preference on such a visual cue since they assign a high probability to the verbal description too.

6 Conclusion

We studied the morphological difference between derived nouns in *-er* and verbs for visual grounding, comparing human judgements with pre-trained Vision and Language models. The dataset we presented allows us to assess vision and language models on their understanding of verbs, deverbal agent nouns, and most importantly the contrast between the two. Our results show that while some models, especially ViLT, show strong results for some of the conceptual domains, they do not support the conclusion that models ground the morphological

Domain	Derived noun	Verb	Morphological contrast
Professional domain	0.76	0.84	0.75
Sport domain	0.69	0.70	0.60
Artistic domain	0.79	0.31	0.51
General	0.92	0.88	0.94
All domains	0.80	0.81	0.78

Table 3: Human judgements: Pearson correlations of judgments for captions containing derived nouns and verbs, and for the difference (contrast).

Model	Derived noun	Verb	Morphological contrast
CLIP ViT-L/14@336px	0.13	0.08	0.15
CLIP RN50x64	0.09	0.08	-0.01
CLIP ViT-B/32	0.09	0.18	0.08
ViLT	0.07	0.26	0.32
LXMERT	0.16	0.03	0.21

Table 4: Human judgments and V&L models overall: Pearson correlations between human judgements and model image-text alignment for captions containing derived nouns, verbs, and the contrast between them.

differences between derived nouns and verbs in a humanlike way.

Highlighting and investigating such a morphological and cognitive difference can refine and improve the alignment of textual and visual input of V&L models. By exploring the visual classification at the morphological level, the aim was to investigate not only the linguistic and morphological influence in the automatic recognition of subjects carrying certain visual information, but also to individuate which architecture of the model better executes the task. In our study, the single-stream ViLT model tends to correlate better with human judgments. Nevertheless, these results are based on a relatively small test set and focus on a restricted set of models, with much scope for further experimentation. In an effort to encourage the community to undertake further investigation of these phenomena, we have shared our code and our dataset text.[1].

[1]https://github.com/ClaudiaTagliaferri/Scenario$_{Refiner.git}$

References

Olivier Bonami and Jana Strnadová. 2019. Paradigm structure and predictability in derivational morphology. *Morphology*, 29(2):167–197.

Emanuele Bugliarello, Ryan Cotterell, Naoaki Okazaki, and Desmond Elliott. 2021. Multimodal pretraining unmasked: A meta-analysis and a unified framework of vision-and-language berts. *Transactions of the Association for Computational Linguistics*, 9:978–994.

Emanuele Bugliarello, Laurent Sartran, Aishwarya Agrawal, Lisa Anne Hendricks, and Aida Nematzadeh. 2023. Measuring progress in fine-grained vision-and-language understanding. *arXiv preprint arXiv:2305.07558*.

Daniela Corbetta. 2021. Effects of typicality and category label on referring expressions in context: Empirical analysis in the domain of "people". *Departament de Traducció i Ciències del Llenguatge*.

Jacob Devlin, Ming-Wei Chang, Kenton Lee, and Kristina Toutanova. 2019. BERT: Pre-training of deep bidirectional transformers for language understanding. In *Proceedings of the 2019 Conference of the North American Chapter of the Association for Computational Linguistics: Human Language Technologies, Volume 1 (Long and Short Papers)*, pages 4171–4186, Minneapolis, Minnesota. Association for Computational Linguistics.

Alexey Dosovitskiy, Lucas Beye, Alexander Kolesnikov, Dirk Weissenborn, Xiaohua Zhai, Thomas Unterthiner, Mostafa Dehghani, Matthias Minderer, Georg Heigold, Sylvain Gelly, Jakob Uszkoreit, and Neil Houlsby. 2020. An image is worth 16x16 words: Transformers for image recognition at scale. *arXiv*, 2010.11929.

Stella Frank, Emanuele Bugliarello, and Desmond Elliott. 2021. Vision-and-language or vision-for-language? on cross-modal influence in multimodal transformers. *arXiv preprint arXiv:2109.04448*.

Eleonora Gualdoni, Thomas Brochhagen, Andreas Mädebach, and Gemma Boleda. 2022a. Horse or pony? visual typicality and lexical frequency affect variability in object naming. *Proceedings of the Society for Computation in Linguistics*, 5(1):241–243.

	Sport domain			Professional domain		
	Deriv. noun	**Verb**	**Morph. contrast**	**Deriv. noun**	**Verb**	**Morph. contrast**
CLIP ViT-L/14@336p	0.02	-0.25	-0.06	-0.04	0.19	0.33
CLIP RN50x64	0.02	-0.31	-0.11	-0.22	0.33	0.23
CLIP ViT-B/32	-0.04	-0.26	-0.11	-0.16	0.23	0.40
ViLT	-0.01	-0.04	0.45	0.30	0.45	0.68
LXMERT	0.08	-0.32	0.17	-0.10	0.18	0.40
	Artistic domain			**General**		
	Derived noun	**Verb**	**Contrast**	**Derived noun**	**Verb**	**Contrast**
CLIP ViT-L/14@336p	-0.03	0.01	0.22	0.28	0.18	-0.06
CLIP RN50x64	0.06	0.21	0.27	0.08	0.23	0.10
CLIP ViT-B/32	-0.09	-0.04	-0.007	0.23	0.25	-0.06
ViLT	0.44	0.15	0.39	-0.06	0.05	0.25
LXMERT	0.29	0.26	0.42	-0.01	-0.25	0.12

Table 5: Human judgement and V&L models by domain: Pearson correlation between human judgments and model image-text matching estimates for captions containing derived nouns, verbs, and the morphological contrast between the derived noun and the verb.

Eleonora Gualdoni, Thomas Brochhagen, Andreas Mädebach, and Gemma Boleda. 2022b. Woman or tennis player? visual typicality and lexical frequency affect variation in object naming. In *Proceedings of the Annual Meeting of the Cognitive Science Society*, volume 44.

Kaiming He, Xiangyu Zhang, Shaoqing Ren, and Jian Sun. 2016. Deep Residual Learning for Image Recognition. In *2016 IEEE Conference on Computer Vision and Pattern Recognition (CVPR)*, pages 770–778, Las Vegas, NV, USA. IEEE.

Lisa Anne Hendricks and Aida Nematzadeh. 2021. Probing image-language transformers for verb understanding. *arXiv preprint arXiv:2106.09141*.

Wonjae Kim, Bokyung Son, and Ildoo Kim. 2021. Vilt: Vision-and-language transformer without convolution or region supervision. In *International Conference on Machine Learning*, pages 5583–5594. PMLR.

Ranjay Krishna, Yuke Zhu, Oliver Groth, Justin Johnson, Kenji Hata, Joshua Kravitz, Stephanie Chen, Yannis Kalantidis, Li-Jia Li, David A Shamma, et al. 2017. Visual genome: Connecting language and vision using crowdsourced dense image annotations. *International journal of computer vision*, 123:32–73.

Tsung-Yi Lin, Michael Maire, Serge J. Belongie, Lubomir D. Bourdev, Ross B. Girshick, James Hays, Pietro Perona, Deva Ramanan, Piotr Doll'a r, and C. Lawrence Zitnick. 2014. Microsoft COCO: common objects in context. *CoRR*, abs/1405.0312.

Letitia Parcalabescu, Michele Cafagna, Lilitta Muradjan, Anette Frank, Iacer Calixto, and Albert Gatt. 2022. VALSE: A task-independent benchmark for vision and language models centered on linguistic phenomena. In *Proceedings of the 60th Annual Meeting of the Association for Computational Linguistics (Volume 1: Long Papers)*, pages 8253–8280, Dublin, Ireland. Association for Computational Linguistics.

Letitia Parcalabescu and Anette Frank. 2022. MM-SHAP: A Performance-agnostic Metric for Measuring Multimodal Contributions in Vision and Language Models & Tasks. ArXiv:2212.08158 [cs].

Letitia Parcalabescu, Albert Gatt, Anette Frank, and Iacer Calixto. 2020. Seeing past words: Testing the cross-modal capabilities of pretrained v&l models on counting tasks. *arXiv preprint arXiv:2012.12352*.

Alec Radford, Jong Wook Kim, Chris Hallacy, Aditya Ramesh, Gabriel Goh, Sandhini Agarwal, Girish Sastry, Amanda Askell, Pamela Mishkin, Jack Clark, et al. 2021. Learning transferable visual models from natural language supervision. In *International conference on machine learning*, pages 8748–8763. PMLR.

Shaoqing Ren, Kaiming He, Ross Girshick, and Jian Sun. 2015. Faster R-CNN: Towards Real-Time Object Detection with Region Proposal Networks. In *Advances in Neural Information Processing Systems 28 (NeurIPS 2015)*, Montreal, Canada.

Hao Tan and Mohit Bansal. 2019. Lxmert: Learning cross-modality encoder representations from transformers. *arXiv preprint arXiv:1908.07490*.

Tristan Thrush, Ryan Jiang, Max Bartolo, Amanpreet Singh, Adina Williams, Douwe Kiela, and Candace Ross. 2022. Winoground: Probing vision and language models for visio-linguistic compositionality. In *Proceedings of the IEEE/CVF Conference on Computer Vision and Pattern Recognition*, pages 5238–5248.

Andrea Tyler and William Nagy. 1989. The acquisition of english derivational morphology. *Journal of Memory and Language*, 28(6):649–667.

A Appendix

Instructions for participants:

Welcome to our survey! Our project focuses on improving existing annotation accompanying pictures. You will be presented with pictures and asked to indicate to which degree you agree with some statements. The study should take you around 15-20 minutes to complete. Your participation in this research will be paid only if you complete the survey. Please make sure to be redirected to Prolific at the end of the survey. In such a way, we can check if you completed the study and pay your participation.The ProlificID and all the sensitive data will be deleted once the payment is done. In the next page, you will be able to read more about the study and how we are doing with the data. If you would like to contact us to receive more information about the annotation project, please c.tagliaferri1@students.uu.nl or d.paperno@uu.nl.

FlowchartQA: The First Large-Scale Benchmark for Reasoning over Flowcharts

Simon Tannert
IMS, Stuttgart
tannersn@ims.uni-stuttgart.de

Marcelo Feighelstein
Technion, Haifa

Jasmina Bogojeska
ZHAW, Zurich

Joseph Shtok
IBM Research, Haifa
josephs@il.ibm.com

Assaf Arbelle
IBM Research, Haifa

Peter W. J. Staar
IBM Research, Zurich

Anika Schumann
IBM Research, Zurich

Jonas Kuhn
IMS, Stuttgart

Leonid Karlinsky
MIT-IBM Research Lab, Cambridge

Abstract

In this paper, we present FlowchartQA, a new and unique large-scale benchmark for visual question answering (VQA) over flowcharts. FlowchartQA comprises close to 1M flowchart images and 6M question-answer pairs, covering various aspects of geometric and topological information contained in the charts. The questions have been carefully balanced to minimize biases. To accompany the proposed benchmark, we present a baseline model and perform comprehensive ablation studies and qualitative analyses to provide a solid foundation for future work. Our experimental results reveal interesting findings and demonstrate the potential of FlowchartQA as a testbed for flowchart understanding, which has been previously absent in the community.

1 Introduction

Flowcharts and other graph-like charts are very valuable sources of information used to intuitively communicate complex processes, guidelines, workflows, systems and algorithms. They contain text, use various shapes such as rectangles, ovals and diamonds and can have directed edges to define sequence or flow, or undirected edges to define relations. Since they are easy to understand by both technical and non-technical people, they are widely used in numerous fields such as science, education, engineering, manufacturing, healthcare, finance, sales and marketing. Machine understanding of such rich visual information would enable easy, focused access to a large amount of relevant valuable data for automated knowledge extraction systems. However, we found that no currently available benchmark / datset offers any large scale data for training / evaluating flowchart understanding models.

Therefore, inspired by recent advances and successes in addressing vision-language problems and the importance that datasets like FigureQA (Kahou et al., 2018), PlotQA (Methani et al., 2020), and DVQA (Kafle et al., 2018) played for developing and evaluating many state-of-the-art approaches for other types of charts (bar, pie, line and scatter plots), we introduce FlowchartQA – a first of its kind benchmark for question answering on flowcharts. It is a large synthetic corpus of 6M question-answer pairs corresponding to 1M flowchart images with corresponding ground truth annotations, created to enable systematic research and development of methods for machine comprehension for this important chart type. More specifically, the final FlowchartQA dataset contains a grayscale plot image of the graph along with all the metadata providing the node positions and labels, the edge positions and labels, the question, the answer and a multiple choice answer. FlowchartQA contains two types of questions over flowcharts, geometric and topological. The code for generating the flowchart images and ground truth data will also be published.

Another focus of this work is the problem of visual QA over flowcharts. To tackle this problem, we present a baseline model that leverages advanced neural architectures, such as transformers and attention mechanisms. The model is designed to integrate both textual and visual modalities of the input data. The effectiveness of the proposed model is demonstrated through evaluation and ablation experiments.

Proceedings of the 1st Workshop on Linguistic Insights from and for Multimodal Language Processing, pages 34–46
September 22, 2023.

The man contributions of our paper are:

1. Large flowchart dataset with ground truth and QA annotations.

2. Code for controlled generation of diverse graph charts coupled with various questions that can potentially be adapted to generate data relevant for a specific target task.

3. A neural baseline approach for the multiple choice visual QA task over flowcharts: based on text transformers and a combination of text and visual transformers.

2 Related Work

2.1 Visual QA Datasets and Algorithms

Generally, visual question-answering (VQA) was developed for natural images (Yu et al., 2017, 2019, 2020), but was recently applied for documents with figures and diagrams. Among the first and important works is FigureQA (Kahou et al., 2018), addressing the task of analysing different types of charts in the documents, by introducing a large synthetic chart dataset for training. This work uses CNN and LSTM architectures to encode image and text and a classifier for (binary) question answers based on these representations.

Another synthetic dataset, focusing on the bar charts, was introduced in DVQA (Kafle et al., 2018); this work also introduced a neural model for question answering on charts, involving again CNN and LSTM and relying on high-quality OCR; in particular it enables to extract tabular data by appropriate sets of questions. Recently, PlotQA (Methani et al., 2020), brought the synthetic graphics closer to real world by using real tabular data to generate the figures for training.

2.2 Multi-modal Transformer-based VQA Architectures

Transformers (Vaswani et al., 2017) recently were used in computer vision as alternatives to CNNs and have been used extensively for vision tasks such as the Vision Transformer (ViT) (Dosovitskiy et al., 2021) In particular, they find applications in VQA domain: Biten et al. (2021) use layout-aware transformers to answer questions by utilizing the scene text in the image, and Minh (2020) integrate BERT (Devlin et al., 2019) for embedding text with convolutional models to represent images.

Another use of a language based model was shown in Luo et al. (2022), where the GPT2 model (Alec et al., 2019) has been used as the decoder to facilitate image captioning tasks. This and other multi-modal architectures integrating Transformers for combined Vision-Language tasks (Su et al., 2020; Lu et al., 2019; Li et al., 2020) have also shown great benefits of such multi-modal Vision-Language models for visual reasoning and question answering. Following this line of research, we use ViT for producing visual representations of the flowchart images in our baseline.

2.3 Charts Analysis and QA

Related to QA on flowcharts is the task of regular chart analysis. Early works addressing automatic chart classification and data extraction (Savva et al., 2011; Al-Zaidy and Giles, 2015), used classical computer vision techniques, such as codebooks obtained by clustering normalized image patches, connected components (for bars), Hough transform (for pies) and OCR. Al-Zaidy and Giles (2015) was extended in Al-Zaidy et al. (2016) to include chart summarization based on the extracted data.

More recently, Poco and Heer (2017); Dai et al. (2018); Cliche et al. (2017) have presented hybrid neural-algorithmic pipelines, performing detection of the graphical objects and extraction of numerical and textual information using OCR, Computer Vision techniques and rules; our approach belongs to this group of methods in terms of its general design. Other lines of work (Liu et al., 2019; Zhou et al., 2021) propose an end-to-end analysis of the charts by a neural network. Zhou et al. (2021) develops an encoder-decoder architecture an attention mechanism for direct data extraction from bar charts by an RNN. Scatter plots are treated in Cliche et al. (2017) by using bounding boxes proposals of a detector for the points, tick marks and values. In Liu et al. (2019) a standard object detector is equipped with a relation network to address the connections between the different chart elements, such as the individual bars, the legend entries and the numerical and label axes; this model is able to produce bar heights and angles of pie segments (for single pie chart), and to match them against the legend entries. In contrast, in the baseline model presented in this paper, we take the more generic approach, learning to answer questions about flowcharts without explicitly modeling the structure of nodes and edges and the graphical variations.

3 Dataset

We introduce a large, novel, synthetic dataset for question answering and reasoning on flowcharts. Our dataset comprises images of flowcharts together with annotations of the underlying data, the bounding boxes and outline polygons of nodes and edges, textual labels and the adjacency matrix of the depicted graph. We also provide questions, answers and multiple choice answer candidates, covering a large number of graph properties.

The dataset creation process is fully automatic which allows us to create large-scale datasets and parameterized so the creation process can be adapted to various different domains. Graphs can be directed or undirected, contain different numbers of nodes and edges, various node and edge styles and textual or numeric edge labels. We generate questions and corresponding answers for each graph from a rich set of templates which can be extended for domain adaptation. The final output contains a grayscale plot image of the graph along with all the metadata providing the node positions and labels, the edge positions and labels, the question, the answer and multiple choice answers. In the following we will describe the generation steps in more detail.

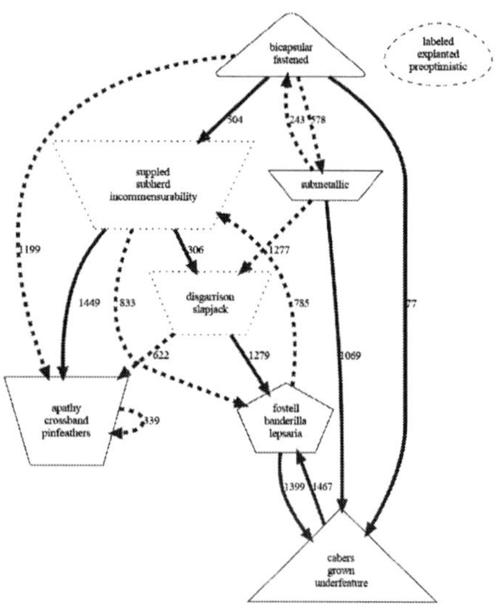

Question	Answer	Answer candidates
How many nodes are in the graph?	8	6, 3, 12, 8, 9
Do all nodes have the same style?	No	Yes, No
Is <submetallic> below <bicapsular\nfastened> on the image?	Yes	Yes, No

Figure 1: Example flowchart image with QA annotations

3.1 Graph Generation

The first step is the generation of a graph which can be parameterized in multiple ways. Among others, we control for the maximum number of nodes and edges in the graph, the maximum degree of each node and whether edges are directed or undirected. Edges can have textual or numeric labels or be unlabeled and nodes and edges can have different styles.

To generate a graph, a random number of nodes is generated within the selected range and node labels are drawn from the provided vocabulary. Edges are then randomly added to the set of nodes according to the constraints given by the generation parameters and edge labels are generated.

The generated graph is laid out and rendered using the graphviz dot engine[1]. We obtain two different versions of the image during rendering, a colored image on which nodes are colored red and edges green and a gray scale image which serves as final output.

3.2 Ground Truth Data

Precise node bounding boxes can be obtained directly as an artefact of the rendering process. Getting ground truth data for edges is more challenging, as they may be curved and intersecting other edges and nodes. From graphviz, we obtain polygons roughly enclosing the edges; for exact binary images depicting the edges we additionally render the flowchart images in color and extract the edgemaps. We provide the bounding boxes obtained from the graph rendering process as ground truth in the dataset.

3.3 QA Generation

For each graph, we generate questions and answers for a large number of question templates that cover a large number of graph properties at different scales as well as node properties and the relations between them. These include binary questions (e.g. `Is <node> in the graph?`, `Do all nodes have the same shape?`, `Is this a directed graph?`), questions with a numerical answer (e.g. `How many nodes are in the graph?`, `What is the eccentricity of <node>?`, `How many strongly connected components are in the graph?`) and questions that can be answered with a node label (e.g. `What is the leftmost node on the image?`, `What is the node with the`

[1] https://graphviz.org/

		Question
geometric	1.	Do all nodes have the same shape?
	2.	Do all nodes have the same style?
	3.	Is <> above <> on the image?
	4.	Is <> below <> on the image?
	5.	Is <> to the left of <> on the image?
	6.	Is <> to the right of <> on the image?
	7.	What is the bottommost node on the image?
	8.	What is the leftmost node on the image?
	9.	What is the rightmost node on the image?
	10.	What is the topmost node on the image?
topological	1.	Are there any two inverted edges?
	2.	Can we reach <> if <> is equal to <>?
	3.	Can we start from any node and arrive at any other node in the graph removing edge <>?
	4.	Do we directly reach <> if <> is equal to <>?
	5.	Does <> connect <> with <>?
	6.	How many edges are in the graph?
	7.	How many neighbors can be reached starting from <>?
	8.	How many nodes are in the graph?
	9.	How many steps are in the shortest path between <> and <>?
	10.	How many strongly connected components are in the graph?
	11.	Is <> connected to <>?
	12.	Is <> directly connected to <>?
	13.	Is it shorter to get from <> to <> if we go through <> than if we go through <>?
	14.	Is <> a direct predecessor of <>?
	15.	Is <> a direct successor of <>?
	16.	Is <> in the graph?
	17.	Is there a node directly connected to itself?
	18.	Is there a path starting from <> and ending at <> using <>?
	19.	Is this a directed graph?
	20.	Is this an undirected graph?
	21.	What is the diameter of the graph?
	22.	What is the eccentricity of <>?
	23.	What is the maximum degree of nodes in the graph?
	24.	What is the node with the maximum degree in the graph?
	25.	What is the radius of the graph?
	26.	What is the state reached if <> is equal to <>?

Table 1: Questions by question type

`maximum degree in the graph?`). We categorize the questions into two categories, *geometric* and *topological*, based on the knowledge required to answer them. The full list of questions can be seen in Table 1. The generated graph is loaded into networkx[2] which allows us to analyze its topology and answer the questions.

[2]https://networkx.org/

3.4 Balancing the Dataset

Due to randomness in the generation process, the resulting dataset can be imbalanced in several ways. Some questions like `How many strongly connected components are in the graph?` are based on features we do not directly control for and will have a different amount of instances per distinct answer. Binary questions have only two answer types while questions that can be answered with a node label have many distinct answers with few instances each.

In order to balance the dataset, we sub-sample the questions and answers in several ways:

1. For questions with a relatively small number of distinct answers (i.e. questions which are not asking for a node label), we subsample the number of instances of each distinct answer to match the one with the least instances. In a second step we subsample the number of instances of each question to the question with the least instances.

2. For questions with many distinct answers (i.e. questions which are answered with a node label), subsample distinct answers until the number of instances matches the question with the least number of instances.

After balancing the dataset, we generate negative answer (i.e. wrong) candidates for multiple-choice question answering. Depending on the question type, we use one of two strategies to sample difficult to answer candidates.

- For questions where the answer is a node label, pick up to n-1 node labels from the same graph.
- For all other questions, sample up to n-1 answers from the space of all answers for that question in the dataset.

Using this strategy, we create a benchmark dataset of 5,964,647 questions and 992,057 images for training, 610,309 questions and 99,284 images for validation and 585,179 questions and 99,139 images for testing. It contains directed and undirected graphs with 8 to 16 nodes and 12 to 24 edges. Nodes styles are either solid rectangles or two or three randomly selected different node styles. Node labels contain one to three words sampled randomly from the vocabulary. Edges are either solid lines or randomly drawn from two different node styles. Edge labels can be empty, numeric or textual in which case they are represented by a single word drawn from the vocabulary.

The number of generated images is evenly distributed across all parameters and the vocabularies of the train, val and test splits are disjunct. We generate up to four negative answers for each question. An example of an image with QA annotations can be seen in Figure 1.

3.5 Real-World Test Set

In order to test our dataset and model further, we also create and provide a small test set from real-world flowcharts. We use a collection of Business Process Model and Notation (BPMN) diagrams[3] which contains user generated diagrams for four different tasks. The data for each task comprises a description of the process to be modeled, multiple diagrams created by users as well as a reference solution.

We generate questions and answers from the task descriptions and node labels using the method from Shakeri et al. (2020). Following the idea in Reddy et al. (2021), we fine-tune BART (Lewis et al., 2020) on the Natural Questions dataset (Kwiatkowski et al., 2019) and extract entities found in the node labels in order to be able to generate a question and answer given a task description and node label as generation cue.

All generated question-answer pairs were manually checked and instances that contain spelling mistakes or syntax errors were removed. The remaining questions and answers were subsampled to reduce the number of duplicates. Using this method, we collect a total of 266 questions over 166 images which we use to evaluate the model we fine-tuned on our synthetic dataset. Unlike the geometric and topological questions in the synthetic dataset, the questions generated from the task descriptions require understanding of the semantics of the flowchart. An example from our real-world test set can be seen in Section D.

4 Baseline Method

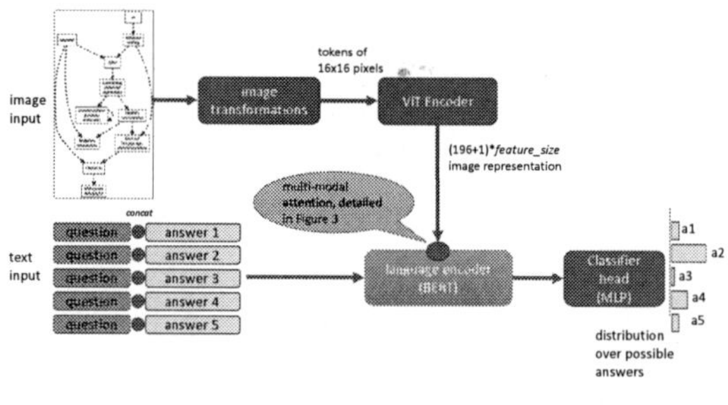

Figure 2: Architecture of our multi-modal baseline. The cross-attention is described in Fig. 3

We fine-tune a multi-modal transformer neural network for multiple choice question answering (cf. Figure 2) to establish baseline performance on our

[3]https://github.com/camunda/bpmn-for-research/

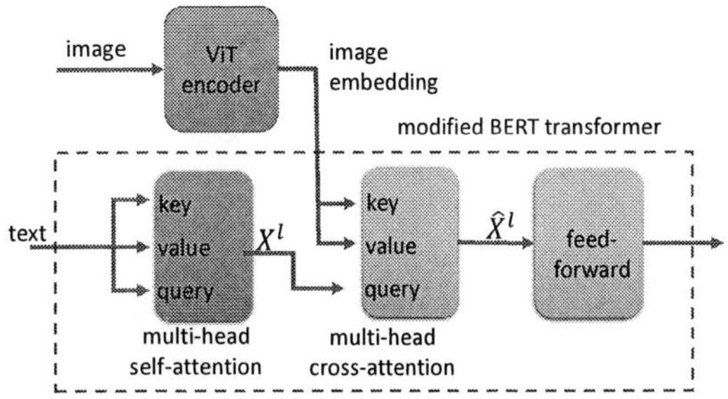

Figure 3: Cross-attention mechanism. A multi-head cross-attention layer is added to each layer of the text classifier to allow it to attend to the features of the visual encoder. The figure depicts the integration into a single layer of the textual encoder.

datasets. Each answer candidate is concatenated with the question and separately encoded by our model using Bert (Devlin et al., 2019). Visual features are extracted from the flowchart image using the Vision Transformer (ViT) (Dosovitskiy et al., 2021) which BERT can attend to during encoding using cross-attention (cf. Figure 3). After encoding, we obtain a probability distribution over the answer candidates using a linear layer.

We also test a variant of this model which does not have access to the flowchart images to test for biases in the questions answer which we refer to as text-only in the results.

4.1 Implementation Details

We use the huggingface library (Wolf et al., 2020) for implementations of the transformer model. The textual encoder model is initialized with pre-trained Bert weights[4] and the visual encoder with pre-trained Vision Transformer weights[5] Each image is rescaled is 224x224 pixels and visual features are extracted from a grid of 14x14 patches. We train our baseline system on the training split for up to three epochs and check performance on a random sample of ten percent of the validation split five times per epoch for early stopping. Training stops early if no improvement is observed in the last three validation runs. Each model was trained with cross entropy loss and Adam optimizer with a learning rate of 10^{-5} and a batch size of 256 on a single NVIDIA RTX A6000 GPU.

[4]https://huggingface.co/bert-base-uncased

[5]https://huggingface.co/google/vit-base-patch16-224-in21k

5 Results

5.1 QA on Synthetic Dataset

The results on the best model configurations can be seen in Table 2 and detailed results for individual questions by question type in Figure 4 and Figure 5, where numbers on the horizontal axes refer to the questions in the geometric category in Table 1.

Question type	Model (Accuracy)		
	Random	Text-only	Multi-modal
geometric	30.91	33.19	71.65
topological	33.22	35.63	74.87
overall	32.58	34.96	73.98

Table 2: Results of the baseline systems by question type

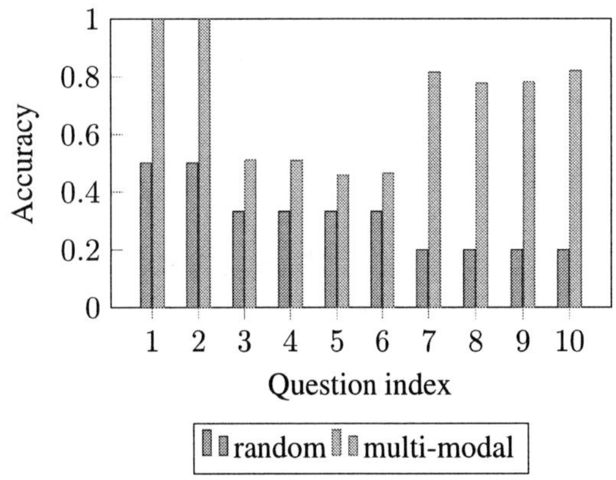

Figure 4: Accuracy of the best performing multi-modal model on the geometric questions.

Figure 6 shows the results of our best-performing multi-modal model in terms of different graph properties. Looking at model performance based on node or edge count, shows that accuracy decreases as the node or edge count increases and the flowcharts become more complex. The effect is more pronounced for the node counts because there are more questions about nodes than there are about edges. The same effect can be observed for the edge label type which does not have a large influence on model performance.

The biggest influence on performance can be observed for the diameter of graphs which drops off significantly for higher diameters as they require better understanding of the graph topology and reasoning capabilities.

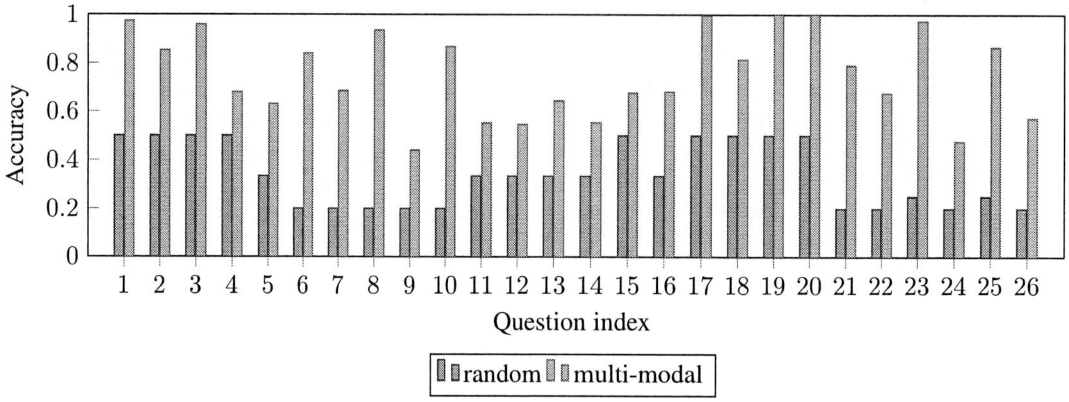

Figure 5: Accuracy of the best performing multi-modal model on the topological questions.

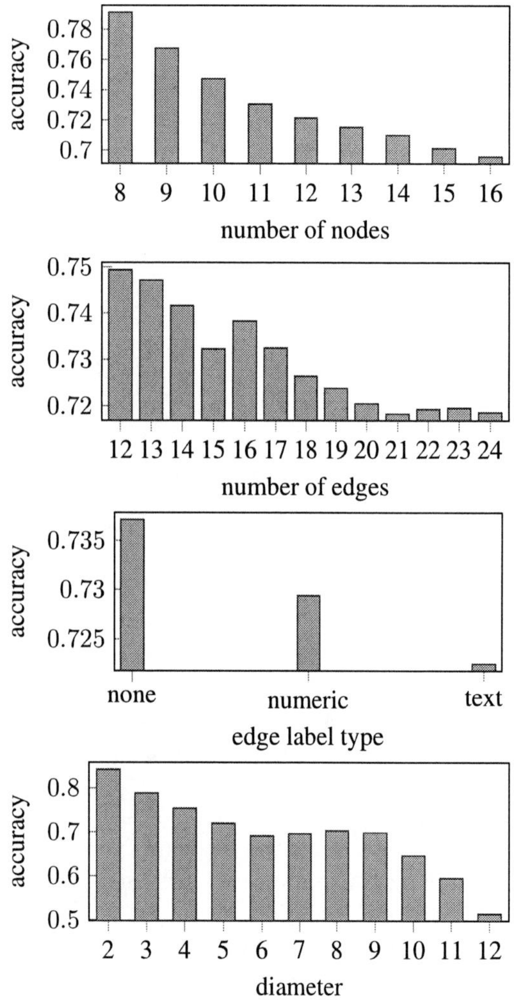

Figure 6: Accuracy of the best-performing multi-modal model on different subsets of the test set. Based on the number of nodes in the flowchart graphs, the number of edges, number of connected components and the diameter of graph with a single connected component.

Dataset	Random	Text-only	Multi-modal	
			frozen	unfrozen
FlowchartQA	32.82	34.96	57.98	73.98
real-world	20.00	21.05	20.68	26.35

Table 3: Results of our model fine-tuned on FlowchartQA, evaluated on the test split of FlowchartQA and our test set of real-world BPMN diagrams (Accuracy).

Question type	Frozen layers (Accuracy)			
	both	visual	textual	unfrozen
geometric	47.14	49.45	57.03	71.65
topological	62.10	62.94	69.21	74.87
overall	57.98	59.22	65.85	73.98

Table 4: Multi-modal model ablation study

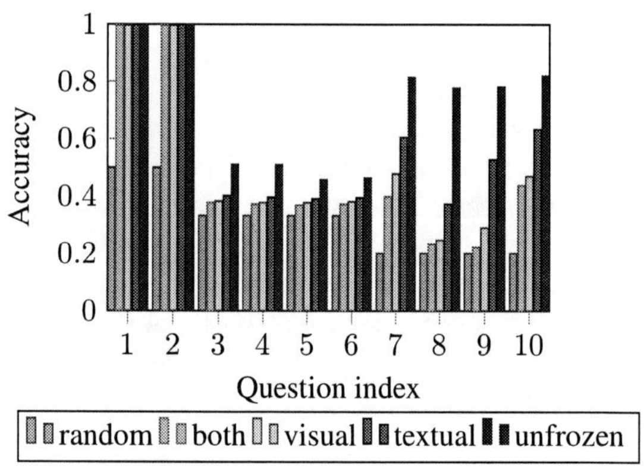

Figure 7: Accuracy of the multi-modal model on the geometric questions with different parts of the model frozen during fine-tuning.

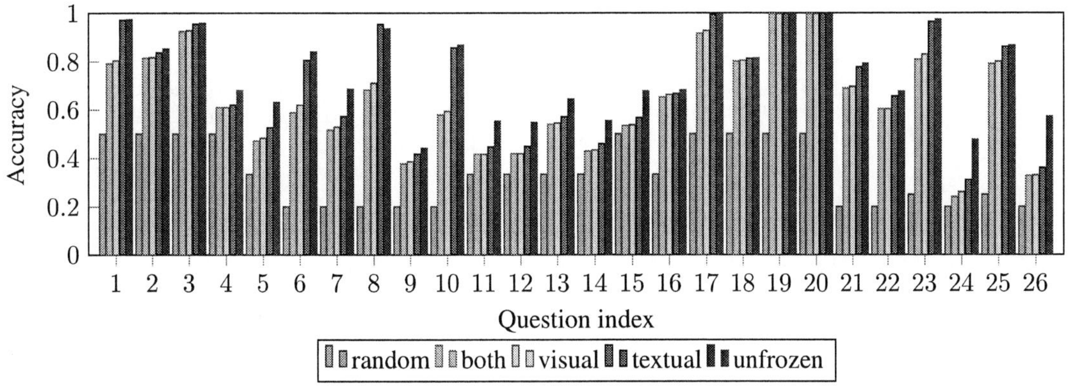

Figure 8: Accuracy of the multi-modal model on the topological questions with different parts of the model frozen during fine-tuning.

5.2 QA on Real-World Test Set

We also evaluate our model on the real-world test set without additional fine-tuning due to the small size of the dataset. The accuracy The results for the real-world dataset in Table 3 show that the model that was fine-tuned with the visual encoder unfrozen leads to an improvement over the random baseline and the text-only model. The model with both visual and textual encoder unfrozen during fine-tuning shows the largest improvement, indicating that it was able to learn generalizable knowledge that transfers to the semantic questions and different visual style of the real-world test set.

6 Ablation Study

We test the influence of keeping different layers of our joint networks frozen during fine-tuning. In the multi-modal baseline, the visual encoder is initialized with pre-trained ViT weights and the text encoder is initialized with Bert weights (cf. Section 4.1). We test the performance of the model while keeping either the visual encoder, the textual encoder or both frozen during fine-tuning. Note that cross-attention and output layers are being trained in all settings because they are not initialized from pre-trained weights.

The results for the multi-modal baseline in Table 4 show that the pre-trained models already exhibit strong baseline performance even when both visual and textual encoder are kept frozen. Fine-tuning the textual encoder only yields a minor improvement in all categories while fine-tuning the visual encoder leads to a stronger improvement over the random baseline. The pre-trained ViT model of the visual encoder was trained on ImageNet-21k (Ridnik et al., 2021) which consists of images depicting natural scenes and seems to benefit from fine-tuning on our graph images. The best performance is observed with both the visual and textual encoder are fine-tuned. This is most notable in the geometric question type which requires spatial reasoning with multiple nodes. Figure 8 breaks down the performance over the different geometric questions. Questions 5.-8. (cf. Table 1) require identifying the top-, bottom-, left- or rightmost node, which benefit noticeably from fine-tuning of the visual encoder. Questions 1.-4. are binary but require identifying and reasoning over two nodes which makes them conceptually more difficult.

7 Conclusions

In conclusion, this paper presents a new benchmark for visual QA over flowcharts, which includes close to 1M synthetic flowchart images and 6M question-answer pairs. The benchmark has been carefully balanced to mitigate biases that could enhance random guess performance. We also provide a baseline model to evaluate the benchmark and demonstrate its performance through both quantitative and qualitative results.

However, the results obtained from the baseline model, which utilizes state-of-the-art computer vision tools, suggest that the QA task on FlowchartQA remains a challenging problem. This presents an interesting opportunity for further exploration by the computer vision community.

Future work directions may include addressing additional tasks, such as the extraction of flowchart components, domain adaption (e.g., biology, chemistry, law, etc.), and extending the tasks and analysis to few-shot or zero-shot question types.

References

Rabah A. Al-Zaidy and C. Lee Giles. Automatic extraction of data from bar charts. *Proceedings of the 8th International Conference on Knowledge Capture, K-CAP 2015*, 2015. doi: 10.1145/2815833.2816956.

Rabah A. Al-Zaidy, Sagnik Ray Choudhury, and C. Lee Giles. Automatic summary generation for scientific data charts. *AAAI Workshop - Technical Report*, WS-16-01 -:658–663, 2016.

Radford Alec, Jeffrey Wu, Rewon Child, David Luan, Dario Amodei, and Ilya Sutskever. Language models are unsupervised multitask learners. In *OpenAI blog*, 2019.

Ali Furkan Biten, Ron Litman, Yusheng Xie, Srikar Appalaraju, and R. Manmatha. Latr: Layout-aware transformer for scene-text vqa., 2021. URL http://arxiv.org/abs/2112.12494.

Mathieu Cliche, David Rosenberg, Dhruv Madeka, and Connie Yee. Scatteract: Automated Extraction of Data from Scatter Plots. *Lecture Notes in Computer Science (including subseries Lecture Notes in Artificial Intelligence and Lecture Notes in Bioinformatics)*, 10534 LNAI(1):135–150, 2017. ISSN 16113349. doi: 10.1007/978-3-319-71249-9{_}9.

Wenjing Dai, Meng Wang, Zhibin Niu, and Jiawan Zhang. Chart decoder: Generating textual and numeric information from chart images automatically. *Journal of Visual Languages and Computing*, 48:101–109, 10 2018. ISSN 1045926X. doi: 10.1016/j.jvlc.2018.08.005.

Jacob Devlin, Ming-Wei Chang, Kenton Lee, and Kristina Toutanova. BERT: Pre-training of Deep Bidirectional Transformers for Language Understanding. In *Proceedings of the 2019 Conference of the North American Chapter of the Association for Computational Linguistics: Human Language Technologies, Volume 1 (Long and Short Papers)*, pages 4171–4186. Association for Computational Linguistics, 2019. doi: 10.18653/v1/N19-1423. URL https://aclanthology.org/N19-1423.

Alexey Dosovitskiy, Lucas Beyer, Alexander Kolesnikov, Dirk Weissenborn, Xiaohua Zhai, Thomas Unterthiner, Mostafa Dehghani, Matthias Minderer, Georg Heigold, Sylvain Gelly, Jakob Uszkoreit, and Neil Houlsby. An Image is Worth 16x16 Words: Transformers for Image Recognition at Scale, 2021. URL http://arxiv.org/abs/2010.11929.

Kushal Kafle, Brian Price, Scott Cohen, and Christopher Kanan. DVQA: Understanding Data Visualizations via Question Answering. In *Proceedings of the IEEE Conference on Computer Vision and Pattern Recognition (CVPR)*, 2018.

Samira Ebrahimi Kahou, Vincent Michalski, Adam Atkinson, Akos Kadar, Adam Trischler, and Yoshua Bengio. FigureQA: An Annotated Figure Dataset for Visual Reasoning, 2018. URL http://arxiv.org/abs/1710.07300.

Tom Kwiatkowski, Jennimaria Palomaki, Olivia Redfield, Michael Collins, Ankur Parikh, Chris Alberti, Danielle Epstein, Illia Polosukhin, Jacob Devlin, Kenton Lee, Kristina Toutanova, Llion Jones, Matthew Kelcey, Ming-Wei Chang, Andrew M. Dai, Jakob Uszkoreit, Quoc Le, and Slav Petrov. Natural questions: A benchmark for question answering research. *Transactions of the Association for Computational Linguistics*, 7:452–466, 2019. doi: 10.1162/tacl_a_00276. URL https://aclanthology.org/Q19-1026.

Mike Lewis, Yinhan Liu, Naman Goyal, Marjan Ghazvininejad, Abdelrahman Mohamed, Omer Levy, Veselin Stoyanov, and Luke Zettlemoyer. BART: Denoising sequence-to-sequence pre-training for natural language generation, translation, and comprehension, July 2020. URL https://aclanthology.org/2020.acl-main.703.

Xiujun Li, Xi Yin, Chunyuan Li, Pengchuan Zhang, Xiaowei Hu, Lei Zhang, and Lijuan Wang et al. Oscar: Object-semantics aligned pre-training for vision-language tasks. In *European Conference on Computer Vision*, pages 121–137, 2020.

Xiaoyi Liu, Diego Klabjan, and Patrick N. Bless. Data extraction from charts via single deep neural network. *arXiv*, 2019. ISSN 23318422.

Jiasen Lu, Dhruv Batra, Devi Parikh, and Stefan Lee. Vilbert: Pretraining task-agnostic visiolinguistic representations for vision-and-language tasks. In *Advances in neural information processing systems*, number 32, 2019.

Ziyang Luo, Yadong Xi, Rongsheng Zhang, and Jing Ma. Vc-gpt: Visual conditioned gpt for end-to-end generative vision-and-language pre-training. In *arXiv:2201.12723*, 2022.

Nitesh Methani, Pritha Ganguly, Mitesh M. Khapra, and Pratyush Kumar. PlotQA: Reasoning over Scientific Plots. In *Proceedings of the IEEE/CVF Winter Conference on Applications of Computer Vision (WACV)*, 2020.

Tung Le; Nguyen Tien Huy; Nguyen Le Minh. Integrating transformer into global and residual image feature extractor in visual question answering for blind people. In *International Conference on Knowledge and Systems Engineering*, 2020.

Jorge Poco and Jeffrey Heer. Reverse-Engineering Visualizations: Recovering Visual Encodings from Chart Images. *Computer Graphics Forum*, 36(3):353–363, 2017. ISSN 14678659. doi: 10.1111/cgf.13193.

Revanth Gangi Reddy, Xilin Rui, Manling Li, Xudong Lin, Haoyang Wen, Jaemin Cho, Lifu Huang, Mohit Bansal, Avirup Sil, Shih-Fu Chang, Alexander Schwing, and Heng Ji. Mumuqa: Multimedia multi-hop news question answering via cross-media knowledge extraction and grounding, 2021. URL https://arxiv.org/abs/2112.10728.

Tal Ridnik, Emanuel Ben-Baruch, Asaf Noy, and Lihi Zelnik. ImageNet-21K Pre-training for the Masses. 1, 2021. URL https://datasets-benchmarks-proceedings.neurips.cc/paper/2021/hash/98f13708210194c475687be6106a3b84-Abstract-round1.html.

Manolis Savva, Nicholas Kong, Arti Chhajta, Fei Fei Li, Maneesh Agrawala, and Jeffrey Heer. ReVision: Automated classification, analysis and redesign of chart images. *UIST'11 - Proceedings of the 24th Annual ACM Symposium on User Interface Software and Technology*, (April):393–402, 2011. doi: 10.1145/2047196.2047247.

Siamak Shakeri, Cicero Nogueira dos Santos, Henghui Zhu, Patrick Ng, Feng Nan, Zhiguo Wang, Ramesh Nallapati, and Bing Xiang. End-to-end synthetic data generation for domain adaptation of question answering systems. In *Proceedings of the 2020 Conference on Empirical Methods in Natural Language Processing (EMNLP)*, pages 5445–5460, Online, November 2020. Association for Computational Linguistics. doi: 10.18653/v1/2020.emnlp-main.439. URL https://aclanthology.org/2020.emnlp-main.439.

Weijie Su, Xizhou Zhu, Yue Cao, Bin Li, Lewei Lu, Furu Wei, and Jifeng Dai. Vl-bert: Pre-training of generic visual-linguistic representations. In *ICLR*, 2020.

Ashish Vaswani, Noam Shazeer, Niki Parmar, Jakob Uszkoreit, Llion Jones, Aidan N Gomez, Łukasz Kaiser, and Illia Polosukhin. Attention is All you Need. In *Advances in Neural Information Processing Systems*, volume 30. Curran Associates, Inc., 2017. URL https://proceedings.neurips.cc/paper/2017/hash/3f5ee243547dee91fbd053c1c4a845aa-Abstract.html.

Thomas Wolf, Lysandre Debut, Victor Sanh, Julien Chaumond, Clement Delangue, Anthony Moi, Pierric Cistac, Tim Rault, Remi Louf, Morgan Funtowicz, Joe Davison, Sam Shleifer, Patrick von Platen, Clara Ma, Yacine Jernite, Julien Plu, Canwen Xu, Teven Le Scao, Sylvain Gugger, Mariama Drame, Quentin Lhoest, and Alexander Rush. Transformers: State-of-the-Art Natural Language Processing. In *Proceedings of the 2020 Conference on Empirical Methods in Natural Language Processing: System Demonstrations*, pages 38–45. Association for Computational Linguistics, 2020. doi: 10.18653/v1/2020.emnlp-demos.6. URL https://aclanthology.org/2020.emnlp-demos.6.

Zhou Yu, Jun Yu, Jianping Fan, and Dacheng Tao. Multi-modal Factorized Bilinear Pooling with Co-attention Learning for Visual Question Answering. In *2017 IEEE International Conference on Computer Vision (ICCV)*, pages 1839–1848. IEEE, 2017. ISBN 978-1-5386-1032-9. doi: 10.1109/ICCV.2017.202. URL http://ieeexplore.ieee.org/document/8237464/.

Zhou Yu, Jun Yu, Yuhao Cui, Dacheng Tao, and Qi Tian. Deep Modular Co-Attention Networks for Visual Question Answering. pages 6281–6290, 2019. URL https://openaccess.thecvf.com/content_CVPR_2019/html/Yu_Deep_Modular_Co-Attention_Networks_for_Visual_Question_Answering_CVPR_2019_paper.html.

Zhou Yu, Yuhao Cui, Jun Yu, Meng Wang, Dacheng Tao, and Qi Tian. Deep Multimodal Neural Architecture Search. In *Proceedings of the 28th ACM International Conference on Multimedia*, pages 3743–3752. Association for Computing Machinery, 2020. ISBN 978-1-4503-7988-5. URL https://doi.org/10.1145/3394171.3413977.

Fangfang Zhou, Yong Zhao, Wenjiang Chen, Yijing Tan, Yaqi Xu, Yi Chen, Chao Liu, and Ying Zhao. Reverse-engineering bar charts using neural networks. *Journal of Visualization*, 24(2):419–435, 2021. ISSN 18758975. doi: 10.1007/s12650-020-00702-6. URL https://doi.org/10.1007/s12650-020-00702-6.

A Appendix

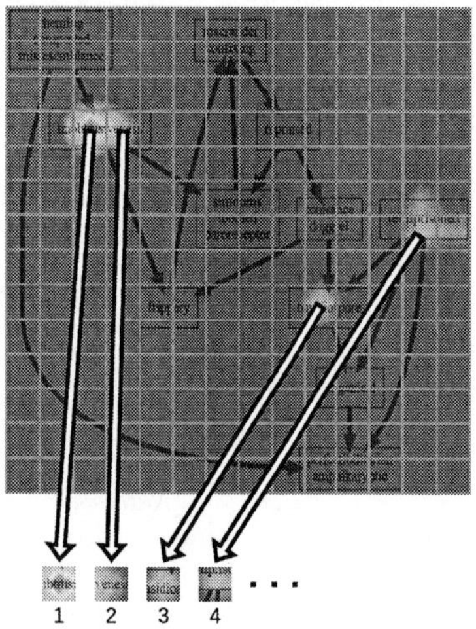

(a) Visualization of the attention ranking method. The heatmap represents the attention allocated to different regions of the image by the visual encoder, the grid represents the segmentation into attention regions (patches corresponding to visual tokens). Regions are ranked based on how much attention they receive and the rank of the region containing the correct answer is determined.

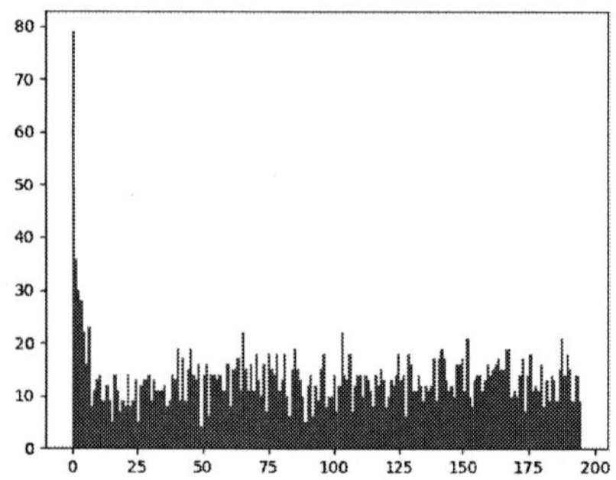

(b) Distribution of the rank of the image region containing the node that correctly answers the question `"What is the node with the maximum degree in the graph?"`

Figure 9: Visual attention analysis

B Quantitative Attention Analysis

For questions that are answered with a node label, we analyze how much attention the region that contains the correct node receives. We rank the regions of the image by how much attention they receive for all instances where they have been answered correctly by the unfrozen multi-modal baseline model. We then determine how much attention the node that answers the question correctly receives by determining the rank of the region that contains the center of the respective node. The rank distribution for `"What is the node with the maximum degree in the graph?"` can be seen in Figure 9b, the rank distributions for questions: `"What is the {topmost, bottommost, leftmost, rightmost} node on the image?"` is shown in Figure 10. In all these figures, ideally, we would like the correct answer to receive the smallest rank possible (aka top rank). The maximal possible rank corresponds to the number of image tokens, $14 \times 14 = 196$ in our case. It is also worth mentioning that model's attention can have multiple uses, sometimes a model can devote a higher attention to a certain region for inhibitory purposes, in other words - to rule out certain options.

The distribution in Figure 9b shows a peak for the top ranks of the attention distribution, indicating that in many instances, the cross-attention allocates most attention on the region that contains the node that answers the question.

The distributions in Figure 10 show that with the exception of `"What is the leftmost node on the image"`, there are also clear peaks near the top ranks of the attention distribution. When we compare this to the relative performance of the models that have layers frozen during fine-tuning (cf. Figure 8), we can see that the model that was fine-tuned with the visual encoder unfrozen yields lower accuracy on `"What is the leftmost node on the image"` (questions number 6) than the other three questions (5, 7 and 8). When we fine-tune with all parts of the model unfrozen the performance degradation vanishes and the other parts of the network make up for a weaker representation in the visual encoder but the effect can still be seen in the visual attention.

C Visual Attention Heatmaps

We attempt to visualize the distribution of question specific attention on the image by aggregating the cross-attention weights and projecting them back onto the image. To do so, we average cross-attention weights across all heads of each layer and multiply the averaged attention weights of all layers. Lastly, we take the attention weights for the `[CLS]` token and normalize the distribution before projecting the weights back on the original image. An example for visualizations on different questions can be found in Figure 11.

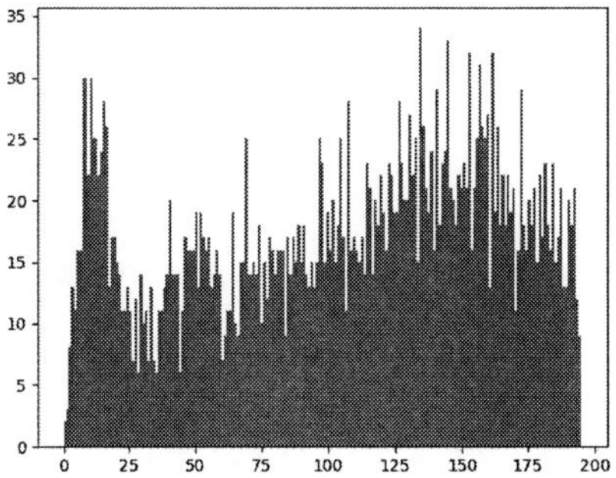

(a) What is the topmost node on the image?

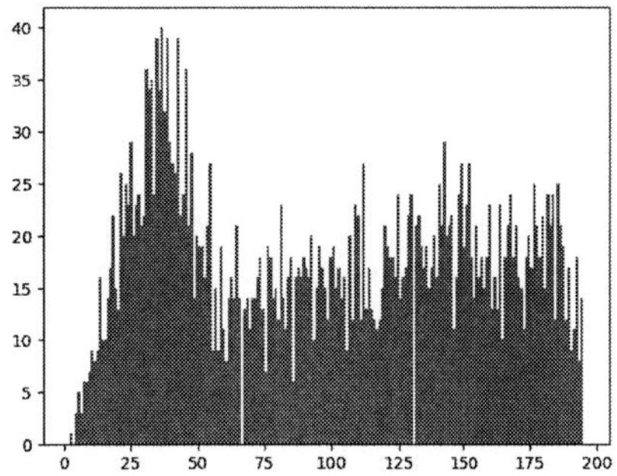

(b) What is the bottommost node on the image?

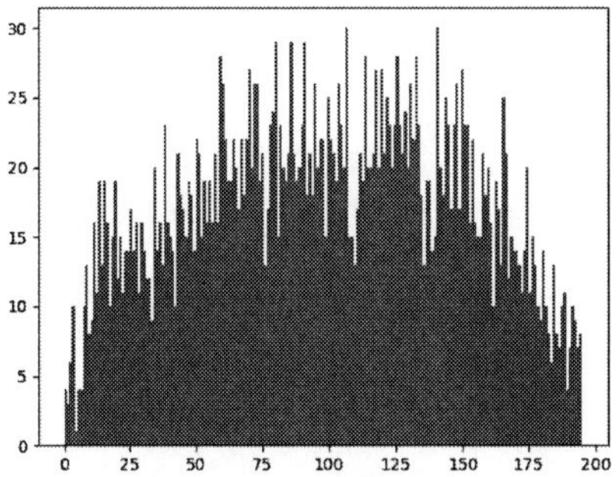

(c) What is the leftmost node on the image?

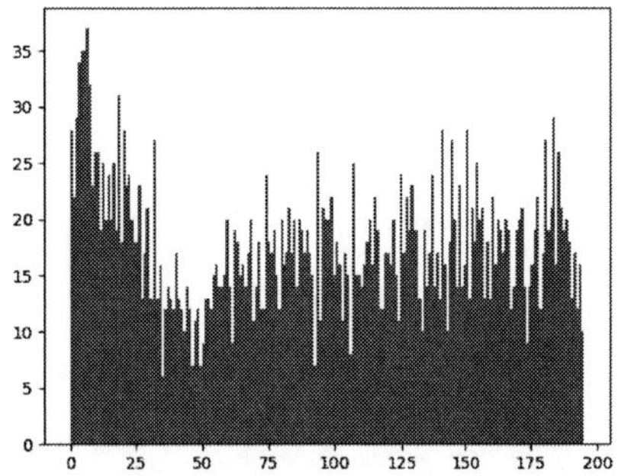

(d) What is the rightmost node on the image?

Figure 10: Distribution of the rank of the image region containing the node that answers the question "`What is the {topmost, bottommost, leftmost, rightmost} node on the image?`"

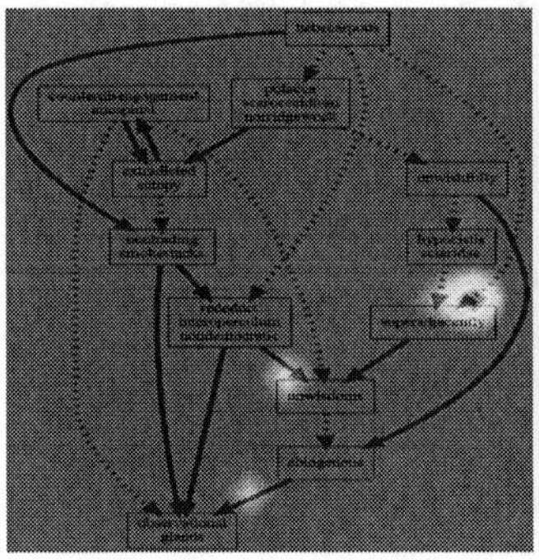

(a) Q: Is this an undirected graph? A: No

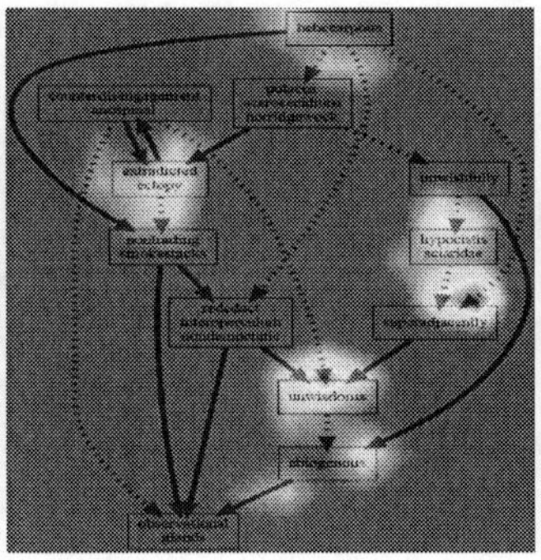

(b) Q: Is there a node directly connected to itself? A: No

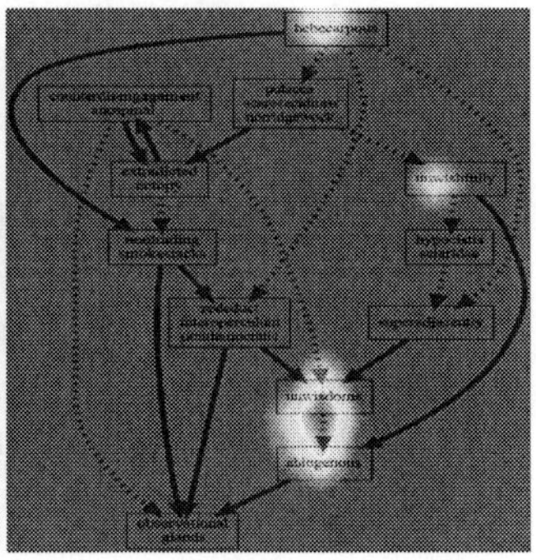

(c) Q: Is <abiogenous> a direct successor of <unwisdoms>? A: Yes

Figure 11: Cross-attention visualization of the multi-modal model.

D Real-World Test Set Example

Figure 12 shows one of the figures from the camunda BPMN dataset that we used to generate the real-world test set as well as the inputs and outputs of our QA generation model. We use the instruction text and a randomly selected node label to generate a question and answer using the model described in Section 3.5. Four negative answer choices are sampled from the node labels of the same diagram.

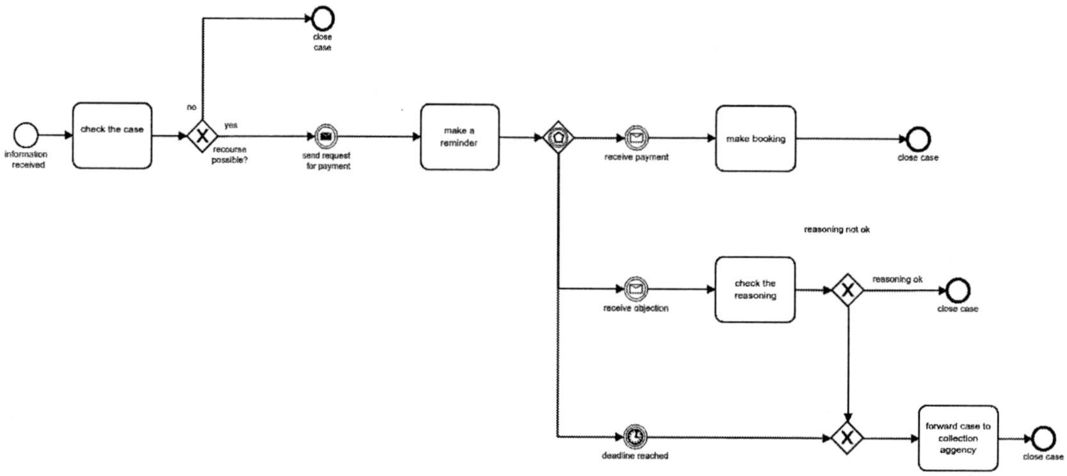

instructions

exercise 3
Recourse
Please model the following process:
If an insurant could be possibly subrogated against, I get information about that. I check that case and if the possibility is really there, I send a request for payment to the insurant and make me a reminder. If recourse is not possible, I close the case.
When we receive the money, I make a booking and close the case. If the insurant disagrees with the recourse, I'll have to check the reasoning of that. If he is right, I simply close the case. If he is wrong, I forward the case to a collection agency.
It the deadline for disagreement is reached and we haven't received any money, I forward the case to the collection agency as well.

Background information:
Insurants can be forced to pay back money they received from the insurance company for different reasons. This is called recourse. Here the clerk describes how this process works.

node label check the reasoning

question when do i check the reasoning of a case?

answers

1. if the deadline for disagreement is reached
2. **if the insurant disagrees with the recourse**
3. if recourse is not possible or money is received
4. if we receive the money
5. if the insurant could be possibly subrogated against

Figure 12: Example BPMN diagram from `https://github.com/camunda/bpmn-for-research` used in the real-world test set together with the instructions provided with the dataset. The extracted node label was used together with the instructions to generate a question and answer. The negative answers were selected from the remaining node labels of the same figure. The correct answer is higlighted in bold.

Presenting an Annotation Pipeline for Fine-grained Linguistic Analyses of Multimodal Corpora

Elena Volkanovska **Sherry Tan** **Changxu Duan**
Debajyoti Paul Chowdhury **Sabine Bartsch**
Technische Universität Darmstadt, Germany
{firstname.lastname}@tu-darmstadt.de

Abstract

With the increasing availability of multimodal documents, it is becoming more difficult for researchers to not only find relevant information within documents in various modalities and media formats, but to also explore potential semantic relationships between data objects of two different modalities embedded in a single document. This paper proposes a method rooted in an annotation pipeline that takes as input text data objects that are either native text objects, or textual descriptions of a multimodal object, such as an image or video, and generates as output an attribute-rich document that unites four levels of annotation in a single framework. The annotated files generated by this pipeline lend themselves to exploration either in a non-programmatic way, by using the Corpus Query Language (CQL) in the web-based graphical user interface (GUI) of the IMS Open Corpus Workbench (CWB), or programmatically, using Python and a Jupyter Notebook. We present some preliminary results of analyses performed on the corpus.

1 Introduction

The means of communicating different areas of knowledge have expanded through the use of different modalities in documents in addition to text, such as images, videos, interactive maps, tables and equations, to name a few. Even documents that do not classify as natively digital content often contain some type of multimodal (MM) data objects. Depending on the genre the document belongs to, MM data objects can serve a range of purposes, from providing additional knowledge to triggering a certain emotional response in the reader (Bednarek and Caple, 2012). Some MM data objects, such as images, may be accompanied by textual descriptions or captions, whose goal is to contextualise the image within the document where it is embedded (Tan et al., 2020).

This paper explores the question of what it takes in terms of corpus annotation to allow for revealing potentially interesting connections between text objects (TOs) of two types: texts of documents (hereinafter: principal text objects, PTOs) and texts that serve as descriptions to multimodal data objects embedded in the document (hereinafter: descriptive text objects, DTOs). We propose an annotation pipeline that integrates existing libraries for natural language processing (NLP) and creates an annotation framework with linguistic and semantic attributes extracted from texts in English, which can be either PTOs or DTOs. The annotation process generates attributes that complement the inherent properties of each document, and allow for performing complex data queries on the document's body text and on texts describing multimodal objects. The attributes are generated at four levels: token, sentence, paragraph, and full-text (document) level. The goal is to create an annotated multimodal corpus with contents in English from a topic area where multimodal objects are natively used to communicate information; one such example is the topic of *climate change*. Thus, the output of the annotation pipeline should satisfy a twofold objective: (1) enriching the corpus with attributes that allow for thorough linguistic exploration of PTOs and DTOs in a non-programmatic manner, using queries performed with the Corpus Query Language (CQL) (Christ, 1994) within CQPweb (Hardie, 2012)[1], and (2) enriching the corpus with linguistic and semantic attributes which can be used to programmatically perform complex analyses on the interaction between text and images using Python and a Jupyter Notebook. Objective (1) should exemplify one way of making data available to researchers who do not necessarily have the skills to use natural language processing (NLP) libraries on a dataset, but who we believe could benefit from insights made available from annotated corpora.

[1] https://cwb.sourceforge.io/

Proceedings of the 1st Workshop on Linguistic Insights from and for Multimodal Language Processing, pages 47–57
September 22, 2023.

2 Related work

Discourse analysis in multimodal contexts is not a novel topic in corpus linguistics. In 1996, Kress and Van Leeuwen (1996) presented a descriptive framework entitled *Grammar of Visual Design*, whose goal was to equip researchers with a tool that would allow them to "read" visual modalities by applying a set of formal rules. The idea was to support efforts to examine the effect data objects in a format other than text, such as images, might have on composing and conveying meaning. Linguists have since approached images in multimodal corpora from several angles, including: (1) analysing and labelling the image itself; (2) conducting linguistic analysis on a caption accompanying the image; (3) simultaneously analysing an image both as a stand-alone artefact and a data object further explained by its caption, and (4) treating image captions as part of the PTO rather than a description of a multimodal object.

Various combinations of the aforementioned approaches can be found in the analysis of austerity discourse in the British press conducted by Tan et al. (2020) using a multimodal image-text corpus. Tan et al. (2020) first categorise images in four superordinate categories, before further classifying them across sixteen subcategories. Images are thus treated as independent data objects that are labeled and categorised as belonging to a certain type; the authors then look into the image-type distribution in the corpus and the associations between image-types and article-types. The analysis of Christiansen et al. (2020) distinguishes between image reference (IR) and image-text reference (ITR). Meanwhile, Bateman and Paris (2020) treat image descriptions, which are essentially DTOs, as part of the PTO when preprocessing the data for their study on changing ideological positions.

Conducting linguistic analysis on texts and captions of images embedded in texts raises the need to preprocess and ingest data in a tool that supports linguistic queries. For example, Griebel et al. (2020) preprocess textual data by annotating it with the Stanford CoreNLP pipeline (Manning et al., 2014), using its processors for tokenization[2], lemmatization, part-of-speech (POS) tagging, and named entity extraction. The linguistic annotation in this case is conducted with a single NLP library, and image captions are pointed to with the markers "captions" and "graphic". Once annotated, the data is ingested in CQPweb and made accessible to researchers of several disciplines.

The applicability of any of these methods for integrating images in discourse analysis driven by corpus linguistics is highly dependent on how images, or any other multimodal objects, are represented in a corpus. For example, an image unaccompanied by a caption cannot in itself be the subject of linguistic analysis, since there is no DTO on which such analysis would be conducted. While devising categories for images allows for both direct interaction with the data and substantial human input in its analysis, this method has limited practicality, since manual categorisation of images is both time- and resource-intensive.

This paper builds on work done by Griebel et al. (2020) and expands the coverage of DTOs to include not only image but also video descriptions. We use the markers "img" for DTOs referring to images and "vid_description" and "vid_summary" for DTOs referring to videos. In addition to presenting the potential for various corpus analyses, the paper elaborates on the steps taken to process the data, since the feasibility of various analyses and the types of questions that may be answered using a given dataset are strongly influenced by decisions made in the data processing stage. This is especially relevant if we take into account that not all researchers can access a corpus programmatically. We propose a linguistic annotation pipeline that uses multiple NLP libraries to extract attributes at token, sentence, paragraph and full-text (document) level. Section 5 showcases how attributes extracted with the linguistic processing pipeline can be used to unlock the potential for conducting corpus analyses both non-programmatically, via CQPweb, and programmatically, with Python and a Jupyter Notebook. Section 6 discusses the benefits and shortcomings of the proposed pipeline, and pinpoints areas for improvement in future work.

3 Corpus

The annotation framework has been developed and tested on the Greenpeace International subcorpus of the InsightsNet Climate Change Corpus (ICCC), a multimodal corpus on climate change described in Volkanovska et al. (2023)[3]. In the ICCC, a docu-

[2] In English texts processed with Stanford CoreNLP, a *token* is usually a word, a number, or a punctuation mark, where the boundary is the white space before and after it.

[3] Permission to use the corpus data for research purposes has been duly obtained.

ment that is *multimodal* would contain data objects in at least one modality that is not natural language text, such as video or image, either embedded in the document text or being referenced by it. The Greenpeace International subcorpus contains documents in English (n=698) from the website of Greenpeace International, of which 446 are documents with embedded images or videos; of these, 375 have images only, 3 have videos only, and 68 have both images and videos. There are 2057 images, of which 1906 are accompanied by a DTO (a caption or an alternative image description), while 151 are not. Of the 123 videos in the corpus, 117 are accompanied by a DTO. Each corpus document contains a set of properties, of which *keywords* and *keyphrases* are of special interest to the annotation pipeline. The corpus has 676879 tokens. The data objects of each document are saved as paragraphs that preserve the original HTML tag and each paragraph's order of appearance in the data source. The data object saved as a paragraph can consist of different modalities, with text, image, and video data objects making up the majority. As such, they stand in the focus of the annotation framework presented in this paper. Anchor links and iframes[4] are also types of paragraphs available in the corpus. Section 5.2 shows how this detailed structure can contribute to gaining various insights from the corpus.

Supplementing the corpus In order to provide a point of comparison and to exemplify better how the approach described in this paper can be used to analyse multimodal data, we supplement the corpus with a dataset that is of the same genre and on the same topic as the Greenpeace International subcorpus. Using the approach employed in the design of ICCC's Greenpeace International subcorpus, we collect multimodal documents on the topic of climate change from the website of the non-governmental organisation (NGO) Climate Analytics[5]. The newly-created dataset has 517 articles, of which 405 are multimodal, with 392 containing images only, one containing videos only, and 12 containing both images and videos. The total number of images is 894, of which 256 are accompanied by a caption. There are video descriptions for 31 of the 33 videos in the corpus. The corpus has 414308 tokens. Anchor links and iframes are accounted for and saved as consecutive paragraphs in the corpus structure, similarly to the Greenpeace International corpus.

[4]An iframe is an element in a webpage that embeds another webpage into the original one. The embedded webpage can also include content from social media, such as Twitter and Instagram posts.

[5]https://climateanalytics.org/

4 Annotation pipeline

As mentioned in Section 1, the annotation framework extracts linguistic and semantic information from a text object, which in this case is either a PTO or a DTO. The annotation pipeline builds on work done in Volkanovska et al. (2023), but entails a clearer delineation between the stages of annotation, generating attributes at four levels of text processing: token, sentence, paragraph, and full-text. Token-level attributes are used as CQL search criteria in CQPweb, while sentence, paragraph, and full-text attributes are utilized in programmatic data analyses.

Document keywords and keyphrases are treated as inherent attributes and used to augment annotation at paragraph, sentence, and token level. The annotation pipeline is implemented as a two-step process, comprised of main annotation and extended annotation. The former generates basic attributes (BA) and derived attributes (DA), while the latter results in extended attributes (EA). Figure 1 gives an overview of the attributes extracted at each level of annotation.

4.1 Main annotation

This section describes the libraries used to implement the main annotation and explains how basic and derived attributes for each annotated text object are obtained.

NLP libraries and processors For the annotation process, some of the NLP libraries applied in previous annotation work were used to extract linguistic attributes and named entities. The libraries include spacy-stanza[6] and Stanford CoreNLP (Manning et al., 2014)[7]. The pipeline includes the following processors: tokenization, part-of-speech (POS) tagging, lemmatization, dependency parsing, and named-entity recognition (NER). We opted for using stanza's models through spaCy's architecture because the latter allows for the application of various language models through a single NLP library.

[6]https://spacy.io/universe/project/spacy-stanza, running on stanza language model 1.4.1

[7]version 4.4.0

Annotation attributes				
	Full-text level	Paragraph level	Sentence level	Token level
BA	Number of tokens Number of words Number of word types Number of content words Named entities	Number of tokens Number of words Number of word types Number of content words Named entities	Number of tokens Number of words Number of word types Number of content words Named entities Sentence index	Token (T) index T start and end character index T lemma T universal POS T Treebank-specific POS T dependency relation T syntactic head (TSH) TSH's lemma TSH's universal POS TSH's treebank-specific POS T morphological features T's NE** IOB code T's NE label
DA	Type-token ratio Lexical density Sentence length* Token length* Word length*	Type-token ratio Lexical density	Type-token ratio Lexical density	
EA	Keywords/keyphrases Abbreviations	Keywords/keyphrases Abbreviations	Keywords/keyphrases Abbreviations	Keywords/keyphrases Abbreviations

BA: Basic Attributes
DA: Derived Attributes
EA: Extended Attributes

*maximum, minimum, median, mean and mode
**named entity

Figure 1: Attributes extracted at each level of annotation

Basic attributes Basic attributes (BAs) are retrieved either directly from the annotation output, or by applying minimum post-processing to it. Minimum post-processing refers to performing simple counts on basic attributes. Figure 1 provides an overview of BAs extracted at each annotation level. For each named entity (NE) at full-text, paragraph and sentence level we extract the properties: NE label, NE text, and frequency and position in the annotated text. At token level, we extract the token's NE inside-outside-beginning (IOB) code, and the token's NE label.

Derived attributes Derived attributes are attributes obtained by performing calculations using the previously extracted BAs at each level of annotation. At **full-text**, **paragraph**, and **sentence** level, we calculate type-token ratio and lexical density. At **full-text** level we also include statistical information about sentence, token, and word length, by calculating the maximum, minimum, median, mean, and mode length values for sentences, tokens and words of the document text.

4.2 Extended annotation

Extended annotation generates custom corpus-relevant attributes and encompasses integration of keywords and keyphrases, which are available for each document of the corpus, in paragraph-, sentence-, and token-level annotation, and extraction of abbreviations. The former is conducted with spaCy's PhraseMatcher tool, while for the latter we used the library SciSpacy (Neumann et al., 2019)[8].

Integration of keyword/keyphrase information Each document of the corpus comes with a set of keywords and keyphrases, which we use to extend the annotations at paragraph, sentence, and token level. At paragraph level, we check if any of the given keywords/keyphrases are present and, if yes, mark their frequency. At sentence level, we annotate the keyword/keyphrase, the index or indices of the token(s) comprising it, and the start and end character index of the respective token(s). At the token level, we add the attribute "keyword" and set it to *yes* or *no* accordingly.

Abbreviation extraction At document and paragraph level, we extract abbreviations, their full form, and their frequency in the annotated text; at sentence level, we extract the token indices, and the start- and end-character index of the abbreviation in addition to its full form. At the token level, we add the attribute "abbreviation" and set it to either *yes* or *no*.

4.3 Saving the annotation pipeline output

The annotation output is saved at several stages of the annotation process. The raw output of the main annotation pipeline is serialized as a pickle file and a spaCy object. Once the basic, derived, and extended attributes are extracted, we save them within

[8]https://github.com/allenai/scispacy

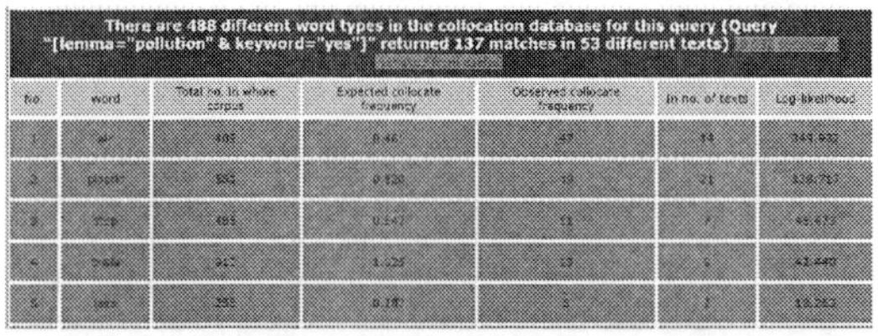

There are 488 different word types in the collocation database for this query (Query "[lemma="pollution" & keyword="yes"]" returned 137 matches in 53 different texts)

No.	word	Total no. in whole corpus	Expected collocate frequency	Observed collocate frequency	In no. of texts	Log-likelihood
1	[illegible]	[illegible]	[illegible]	[illegible]	[illegible]	[illegible]
2	[illegible]	[illegible]	[illegible]	[illegible]	[illegible]	[illegible]
3	[illegible]	[illegible]	[illegible]	[illegible]	[illegible]	[illegible]
4	[illegible]	[illegible]	[illegible]	[illegible]	[illegible]	[illegible]
5	[illegible]	[illegible]	[illegible]	[illegible]	[illegible]	[illegible]

(a)

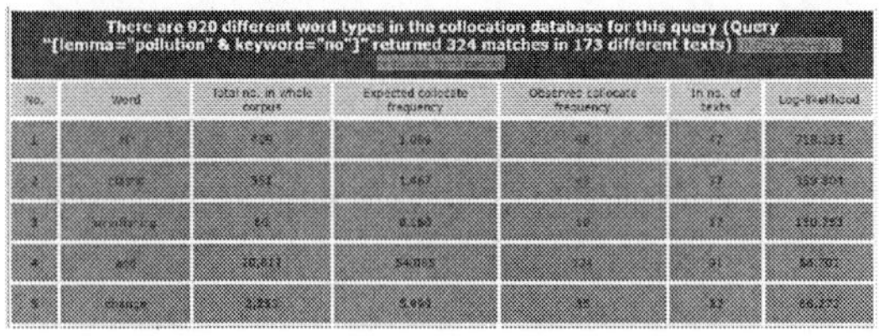

There are 920 different word types in the collocation database for this query (Query "[lemma="pollution" & keyword="no"]" returned 324 matches in 173 different texts)

No.	Word	Total no. in whole corpus	Expected collocate frequency	Observed collocate frequency	In no. of texts	Log-likelihood
1	[illegible]	[illegible]	[illegible]	[illegible]	[illegible]	[illegible]
2	[illegible]	[illegible]	[illegible]	[illegible]	[illegible]	[illegible]
3	[illegible]	[illegible]	[illegible]	[illegible]	[illegible]	[illegible]
4	[illegible]	[illegible]	[illegible]	[illegible]	[illegible]	[illegible]
5	[illegible]	[illegible]	[illegible]	[illegible]	[illegible]	[illegible]

(b)

Figure 2: Collocations of the term *pollution* when the term is a keyword (2a) and when it is not a keyword (2b) in Greenpeace International.

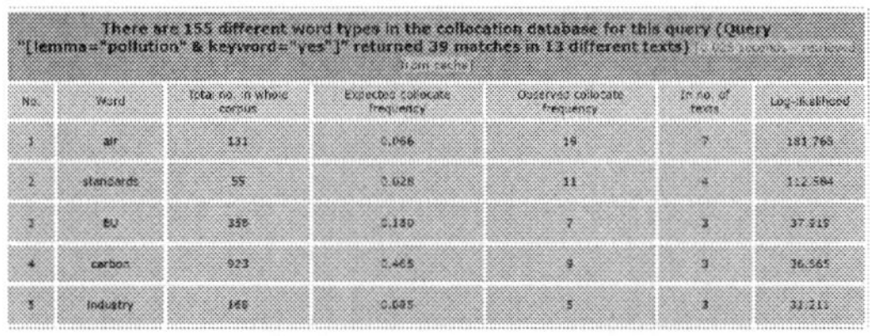

There are 155 different word types in the collocation database for this query (Query "[lemma="pollution" & keyword="yes"]" returned 39 matches in 13 different texts)

No.	Word	Total no. in whole corpus	Expected collocate frequency	Observed collocate frequency	In no. of texts	Log-likelihood
1	air	131	0.066	19	7	181.768
2	standards	55	0.028	11	4	112.584
3	EU	358	0.180	7	3	37.919
4	carbon	923	0.465	9	3	36.565
5	industry	168	0.085	5	3	31.211

(a)

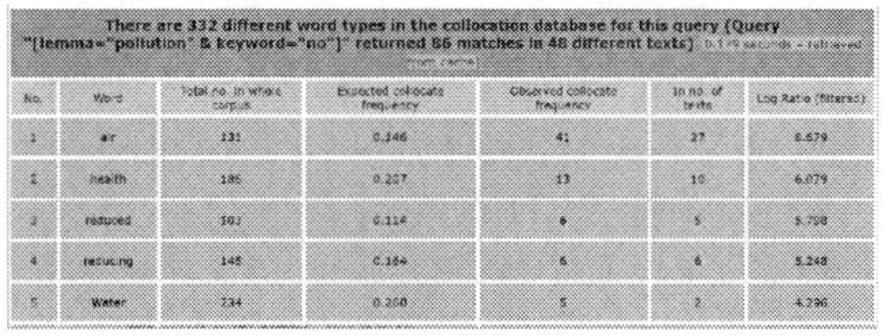

There are 332 different word types in the collocation database for this query (Query "[lemma="pollution" & keyword="no"]" returned 86 matches in 48 different texts)

No.	Word	Total no. in whole corpus	Expected collocate frequency	Observed collocate frequency	In no. of texts	Log Ratio (filtered)
1	air	131	0.146	41	27	8.679
2	health	186	0.207	13	10	6.079
3	reduced	103	0.114	6	5	5.798
4	reducing	145	0.164	6	6	5.248
5	Water	234	0.260	5	2	4.296

(b)

Figure 3: Collocations of the term *pollution* when the term is a keyword (3a) and when it is not a keyword (3b) in Climate Analytics.

the corpus document under the key *annotated content* and export the complete output as a JSON file. This file serves as a repository containing the attributes at all four levels and as such represents a source file from which files in a CQPweb-specific format can be easily created.

5 Use cases

This section exemplifies how the attributes extracted with the annotation pipeline of Section 4 can be used for performing corpus queries with the CQL and CQPweb, or to conduct deeper corpus exploration with Python and a Jupyter Notebook.

5.1 Corpus exploration with CQPweb

The annotation pipeline described in Section 4 generates an annotated corpus in a format suitable for ingestion and indexing with CQPweb [9]. According to Davies (2005), the option to query large collections of data with extensive annotations using CQL via CQPweb makes CQPweb a powerful query tool. Search queries with CQPweb can be simple, when a user enters a search term or phrase in a similar way as one would in any of the popular search engines, such as *pollute* or *forest fires*, or complex, when queries are defined with CQL using the token-level attributes listed in the column "Token level" of Figure 1. Results can be returned in different formats, such as Key Word in Context (KWiC) concordances, word frequency lists, or collocation tables. The wider textual context of the search query can also be retrieved for further examination. The objective of this use case is to test whether the detailed and extended token attributes can be indexed and searched with CQPweb, and whether we can distinguish between queries done on PTOs and DTOs.

With the basic token-level attributes listed in Section 4 and CQL, researchers can explore questions such as *Which organisations have been explicitly named as culprits of pollution in this corpus?* by extracting all sentences where the verb *pollute* is the syntactic head of a named entity with the label *ORG*[10], whose dependency relation to the verb *pollute* is that of a nominal subject[11], [12]. Another query along these lines would be to compare the number of passive sentences associated with the verb *pollute* in which the passive agent is explicitly stated to the number of agentless passive sentences. Such a query could shed a light on the circumstances in which the agent of a passive sentence is omitted[13]. Using the above-mentioned queries, we found that in the Greenpeace International corpus, only one organisation, Glencore, was openly mentioned as an organisation polluting the environment.

[9]CQPweb v3.3.17

[10]organisation

[11]CQL query: [entType="ORG" & dep="nsubj" & headLemma="pollute"]

[12]It should be borne in mind that linguistic features are extracted automatically, and careful examination of the output is necessary before making definitive claims or conclusions.

[13]CQL query for all passive sentences (1) and for passive sentences in which the agent is mentioned (2): (1) [dep="aux:pass" & headLemma="pollute"]; (2) [dep="aux:pass" & headLemma="pollute"][]*[dep="obl:agent"]

The query did not return any results from the Climate Analytics corpus. Greenpeace International had five passive sentences with the verb *pollute*, which were all agentless. Climate Analytics had three passive sentences with the same verb, which were also agentless.

Using a combination of basic and extended token-level attributes, we compare the collocates of the word *pollution* in documents in which it has been labelled as a keyword, against its collocates in documents where it is not a keyword. This can be done with CQL queries[14] and CQPweb's built-in collocation finder, which allows us to examine the queried term's collocates using one of the eight available association measures[15]. These queries can be conducted on PTOs or on DTOs; for the latter, we would need to add *within img*, *within vid_description* or *within vid_summary* in the CQL query[16]. When *pollution* is a keyword in Greenpeace International, its top-five collocates are *air, plastic, stop, crisis, less*; when it is not a keyword, it collocates with *air, plastic, overfishing, and, change.* In Climate Analytics, *pollution* as a keyword collocates with *air, standards, EU, carbon, industry* and as a non-keyword with *air, health, reduced, reducing, water.* Figures 2a and 2b, and 3a and 3b provide an overview of the query output from Greenpeace International and Climate Analytics respectively.

5.2 Corpus exploration with Python and a Jupyter Notebook

The structure yielded by the annotation pipeline described in Section 4 along with the metadata provided by the ICCC, combined into a JSON file, allows for corpus exploration by applying programmatic methods. Combining metadata and annotations can help researchers to quickly get an overview of the average statistical information contained in the DA of the annotation as well as a general overview of the metadata information; such as a plot containing years and the frequency of articles. The goal of having such a tool is to allow users to answer questions such as: *What are the keywords/keyphrases involved in Greenpeace International articles versus Climate Analytics articles in the years between 2019 and 2020? And which of those keywords/keyphrases appear in image or video DTOs and what is the link to the image/video?* Such a query is made possible by the annotation attributes and the embedded corpus structure. To answer the first question, one can count the number of keyword/keyphrase occurrences in documents belonging to the specified years of publication and compare the differences between the respective documents from each corpus, as seen in Figure 4.

The second question can be answered by choosing one of the keywords/keyphrases shown in Figure 4 and looking for the specific keyword/keyphrase that was annotated in image and video DTOs. The result with the example keyphrase *climate change* can be seen in Appendix A. The user is able to view the unique filename, the multimodal data type (image, video description or video summary), the paragraph text in which the keyphrase appears and the link to view the image or the video.

The same type of analysis can be done with the extracted entities. Figure 5 shows the comparison between organisations extracted in Greenpeace International and Climate Analytics. If the user is interested, a list of contexts where a specific entity occurs can also be obtained similar to that of Appendix A.

Accessing anchor links and iframe objects Multimodal data objects embedded in a document, such as images and videos, are usually accompanied by captions or video transcriptions. However, data that are obtained from the web, such as the corpora that are being explored in this paper, may also contain other types of data objects, such as anchor links and iframes, embedded in a document's text. These data objects are usually tricky to query as they are not accompanied by textual data of their own. One way to solve this problem would be to query for anchor links and iframes based on their context text; implying that when an anchor link or an iframe is found between two text paragraphs, it is likely that they are related to the context text rather than being standalone corpus elements. Such a query can be made possible due to the structure of the annotation and the preserved order of the data objects in which the document was obtained from the web. Another more general way to query would be to take all documents in the Greenpeace Interna-

[14] CQL queries: [lemma="pollution" & keyword="yes"], [lemma="pollution" & keyword="no"]

[15] Mutual information, MI3, Z-score, T-score, Log-likelihood, Dice-coefficient, Log-Ratio (filtered), and Conservative LR

[16] CQL query: [lemma="pollution" & keyword="yes"] within img ("img" can be replaced with "vid_description" or "vid_summary" depending on the DTO of interest).

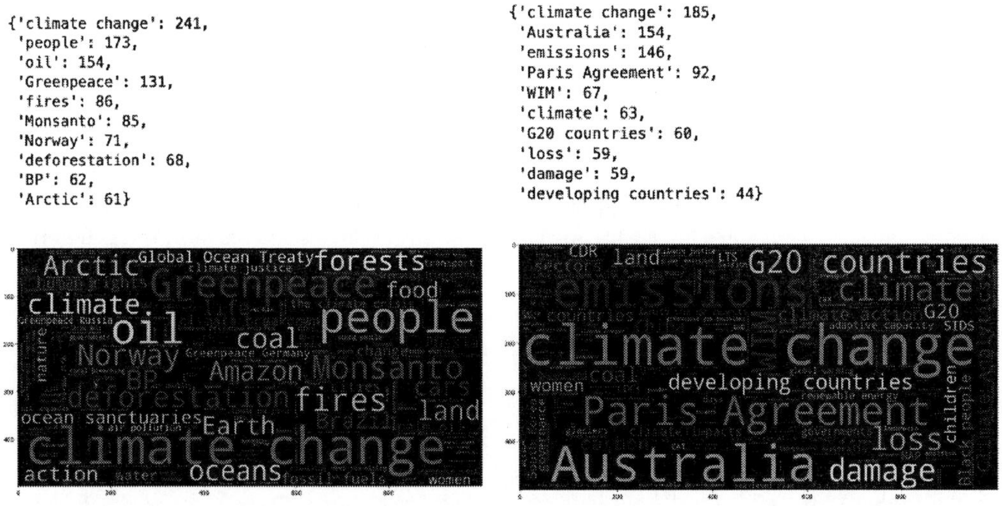

Figure 4: Keyword/keyphrase comparison between Greenpeace International (left) and Climate Analytics (right) between the years 2019 and 2020 with top 10 keywords/keyphrases and their frequencies.

Figure 5: Entity: ORG comparison between Greenpeace International subcorpora (left) and Climate Analytics (right) between the years 2019 and 2020.

tional subcorpus with a specific keyword/keyphrase (e.g. *climate change*) within a specific year (e.g. 2019 and 2020). The tool will yield a list of anchor and iframe links and their corresponding contextual texts that satisfy the query requirements (see Appendix B for example output).

6 Conclusions

This paper demonstrates how a linguistic annotation pipeline can be applied to a multimodal corpus containing text, images, and videos, where images and videos are accompanied by textual descriptions, and how the attributes generated at various stages of annotation can support corpus analyses. Rather than introducing modality-specific attributes, the pipeline extends linguistic annotations to given descriptions of image and video data objects, thus making them accessible through the same query approach used for a document's text. We also show how a dataset annotated using our pipeline can be made available to researchers who are familiar with corpus querying techniques, but possess limited programming skills. In this section, we give a brief overview on some of the lessons learned during the annotation process, and how these can pave the way for future research in this field.

NLP researchers working with English texts have a myriad of NLP libraries at their disposal. Annotating a corpus by combining several NLP tools could generate a highly-detailed profile of a dataset, with many attributes to be used as query criteria. However, neither combining NLP tools nor making token-level attributes accessible is an easy task. For example, NLP tools could employ various tokenizers with differing interpretations of what a token is. In the context of our study, it proved challenging to reap the benefits of some Transformer-based language processing tools, whose success in tackling unseen words is to an extent due to the use of subword units[17]. In the future, we would like to explore ways of integrating annotations obtained with Transformer-based NLP libraries in the available token-level attributes. Having data of a certain size is also paramount to performing analyses. In Section 5.1 we attempted to compare the number of passive sentences with and without an agent involving a specific verb, but did not manage to retrieve a representative number of examples to analyse further due to the relatively small size of our corpus. This proved that the more fine-grained a query is, the more important the size of the corpus becomes. Finally, future work might consider storing metadata information about the annotation pipeline presented in this paper in formats that could promote the pipeline's integration in existing collections of tools for natural language processing[18].

7 Limitations

This paper presents a complex annotation framework that might not translate well into languages with fewer processing resources. It is highly likely that this type of linguistic analysis would not be fully reproducible for low-resource languages, which poses a hindrance to the transferability of this methodology at least in its full scope.

In Section 3 it was underscored that the annotation framework is only applicable to multimodal objects (images and videos) accompanied by textual descriptions. There is a marginal number of instances in which such descriptions were not readily available; consequently, it would not be possible to integrate these objects in the final analysis. This limitation could be overcome by applying image and video captioning tools, or by introducing modality-specific attributes, such as the output of object recognition techniques for images and videos. However, this is a layer of data processing that is beyond the scope of this paper.

The annotation pipeline was executed on a dedicated Nvidia GPU server. The annotation of the two corpora took approximately 360 minutes to run. The development and the running of the pipeline proved to be a computationally expensive process, which makes it potentially forbidding for researchers with limited access to such resources.

In Section 4.3 it is mentioned that the raw output of NLP libraries is serialized for the purpose of ensuring reusability of annotated texts. Loading serialized files in the respective NLP libraries and extracting additional attributes is dependent on the availability of the same version of the language model that was used in the NLP library that generated the serialized file. This could pose a limitation to reusability should the same language model no longer be available.

[17] For example, Devlin et al. (2019) use wordpieces, which are neither purely word-based nor character-based units

[18] One such example would be the XML Metadata Interchange (XMI), which is in use in DKPro, a community of projects for re-usable NLP pipelines.

Ethics Statement

An ethical consideration in this research was respecting and duly acknowledging the rights of owners of data and resources. This meant observing the conditions laid out in copyright regulations governing usage of the contents stipulated by the entity holding intellectual property rights over the data. It is necessary to point out that various data holders may apply differing constraints on data use, especially with regard to text on the one hand, and multimodal file formats on the other.

We acknowledge that using GPU computing leaves a carbon footprint. While this study does not include a training step, as is the case with the development of large language models (LLMs), we recognise the environmental consequences of GPU usage and commit to using these resources responsibly.

References

John A Bateman and Cécile L Paris. 2020. Searching for 'austerity': Using semantic shifts in word embeddings as indicators of changing ideological positions. In *Multimodal Approaches to Media Discourses*, pages 11–41. Routledge.

Monika Bednarek and Helen Caple. 2012. *News discourse*, volume 46. A&C Black.

Oliver Christ. 1994. A modular and flexible architecture for an integrated corpus query system. In *Proceedings of COMPLEX'94: 3rd Conference on Computational Lexicography and Text Research*, pages 23–32, Budapest, Hungary. tt cmp-lg: tt 9408005.

Alex Christiansen, William Dance, and Alexander Wild. 2020. Constructing corpora from images and text. *Corpus approaches to social media*, pages 149–174.

Mark Davies. 2005. The advantage of using relational databases for large corpora: Speed, advanced queries, and unlimited annotation. *International Journal of Corpus Linguistics*, 10:307–334.

Jacob Devlin, Ming-Wei Chang, Kenton Lee, and Kristina Toutanova. 2019. BERT: Pre-training of deep bidirectional transformers for language understanding. In *Proceedings of the 2019 Conference of the North American Chapter of the Association for Computational Linguistics: Human Language Technologies, Volume 1 (Long and Short Papers)*, pages 4171–4186, Minneapolis, Minnesota. Association for Computational Linguistics.

Tim Griebel, Stefan Evert, and Philipp Heinrich. 2020. *Multimodal approaches to media discourses: Reconstructing the age of austerity in the United Kingdom*. Routledge.

Andrew Hardie. 2012. CQPWeb—combining power, flexibility and usability in a corpus analysis tool. *International Journal of Corpus Linguistics*, 17(3):380–409.

Gunther R Kress and Theo Van Leeuwen. 1996. *Reading images: The grammar of visual design*. Psychology Press.

Christopher D Manning, Mihai Surdeanu, John Bauer, Jenny Rose Finkel, Steven Bethard, and David McClosky. 2014. The Stanford CoreNLP natural language processing toolkit. In *Proceedings of 52nd annual meeting of the association for computational linguistics: system demonstrations*, pages 55–60.

Mark Neumann, Daniel King, Iz Beltagy, and Waleed Ammar. 2019. ScispaCy: Fast and Robust Models for Biomedical Natural Language Processing. In *Proceedings of the 18th BioNLP Workshop and Shared Task*, pages 319–327, Florence, Italy. Association for Computational Linguistics.

Sabine Tan, Kay O'Halloran, Peter Wignell, and Katharina Lobinger. 2020. Images of austerity in the british press and in online media. *Multimodal Approaches to Media Discourses: Reconstructing the Age of Austerity in the United Kingdom*, pages 134–62.

Elena Volkanovska, Sherry Tan, Changxu Duan, Sabine Bartsch, and Wolfgang Stille. 2023. The InsightsNet Climate Change Corpus (ICCC). *BTW 2023*.

Appendix

A Keyword/keyphrase in context with links to multimodal objects

```
cc_gp_int_204 img Hundreds of young protesters march through Central Tokyo to demand urgent action to prevent
climate change (November 2019). The demonstration is part of the global movement known as Fridays for Future.
 https://www.greenpeace.org/static/planet4-international-stateless/2020/04/bf786b62-gp0stugqt_medium_res_with
_credit_line-1024x736.jpg
cc_gp_int_314 img SYDNEY, AUSTRALIA - MARCH 15: Protesters during a Climate Change Awareness March on March 1
5, 2019 outside Sydney Town Hall, Australia. The protests are part of a global climate strike, urging politic
ians to take urgent action on climate change. James Gourley/Getty Images
 https://www.greenpeace.org/static/planet4-international-stateless/2019/03/2dd60f1c-gettyimages-1135884196.jp
g
cc_gp_int_314 img PARIS, FRANCE - MARCH 16: A protester holds a sign reading "Game over" as he takes part in
the "March of The Century" (La Marche du Siecle) to demand answers to climate change on March 16, 2019 in Par
is, France. Several thousand people demonstrated in Paris to denounce the government's inaction on climate. C
hesnot/Getty Images
 https://www.greenpeace.org/static/planet4-international-stateless/2019/03/4cbe4794-gettyimages-1136214712.jp
g
cc_gp_int_314 img TOKYO, JAPAN - MARCH 15: Participants hold signs and shout slogans during the Fridays for F
uture march on March 15, 2019 in Tokyo, Japan. Students around the world took to the streets on March 15 to p
rotest a lack of climate awareness and demand that elected officials take action on climate change. Inspired
by Greta Thunberg, the 16-year-old environmental activist who started skipping school since August 2018 to pr
otest outside Sweden's parliament, school and university students worldwide have followed her lead and shared
her alarm and anger. Takashi Aoyama/Getty Images
 https://www.greenpeace.org/static/planet4-international-stateless/2019/03/5be5f84d-gettyimages-1135912723.jp
g
cc_gp_int_402 img Thousands of Belgian students, for the seventh Thursday in a row, march through Brussels in
order to draw attention to climate change.
 https://www.greenpeace.org/static/planet4-international-stateless/2019/08/b08d4d69-gp0stt1dd_medium_res.jpg
cc_gp_int_402 img In a peaceful protest Greenpeace activists from Norway, Sweden, Denmark and Germany climb t
he oil rig West Hercules, located near Rypefjord village in the north of Norway, and display a banner reading
"Ban New Oil". While a growing movement calling for real action on climate change is happening all over the w
orld, Equinor's rig is preparing for a season of oil drilling in the Arctic waters of the Barents Sea.
 https://www.greenpeace.org/static/planet4-international-stateless/2019/08/923c5b21-gp0stt9g6_medium_res.jpg
```

Figure 6: Keyphrase *climate change* in Greenpeace International subcorpus with corresponding links to multimodal objects for the years 2019 and 2020.

```
cc_ca_en_28 img Rural communities in the Horn of Africa Drylands like these farmers in Eritrea, depend on sea
sonal rainfall to sustain agriculture and are especially vulnerable to droughts which are becoming more sever
e due to climate change.
 https://climateanalytics.org/images/w693/africa-2363380_1920.jpg
cc_ca_en_371 video -description In this webinar, the second in a series on land-climate interactions under th
e LAMACLIMA project, Dr Wim Thiery of the Vrije Universiteit Brussel (VUB) and Kashif Salik of the Sustainabl
e Development Policy Institute (SDPI) provide insights into irrigation's effect on climate change and its ben
efits and trade-offs for local people, and discuss how LAMACLIMA, a European research project coordinated by
Climate Analytics, seeks to inform the drafting of sustainable land-based adaptation and mitigation measures.
 https://youtu.be/lQqvzOudNwE
cc_ca_en_382 video -summary I really want to understand what could be really helpful in tackling climate chan
ge versus what could actually just be greenwashing .
 https://www.youtube-nocookie.com/embed/8i6FZqJD_mQ
cc_ca_en_382 video -summary I'm angry that some governments aren't taking their responsibilities for climate
change seriously seriously .
 https://www.youtube-nocookie.com/embed/8i6FZqJD_mQ
cc_ca_en_382 video -description Climate Analytics celebrates International Women's Day - Jessie Schleypen and
Dr Anne Zimmer are economists, looking at climate change from different angles.
 https://www.youtube-nocookie.com/embed/nvZHKtQEeIw
cc_ca_en_382 video -description Here, they tell us in their own language (Filipino and German) about their wo
rk providing evidence to persuade governments that tackling climate change is both necessary and in their own
interest.
 https://www.youtube-nocookie.com/embed/nvZHKtQEeIw
cc_ca_en_382 video -summary  developing countries have done the least to cause climate change but have the le
ast means to deal with its impacts .
 https://www.youtube-nocookie.com/embed/-ei3fUsqxi0
cc_ca_en_382 video -summary Many of those countries have ambitious climate plans to help them to develop sust
ainably well adapt into the embeds of climate change so they must not face any challenge while trying to acce
ss resources from the different climate funds .
 https://www.youtube-nocookie.com/embed/-ei3fUsqxi0
```

Figure 7: Keyphrase *climate change* in Climate Analytics subcorpus with corresponding links to multimodal objects for the years 2019 and 2020.

B Anchor links and iframes with contexual text

```
cc_gp_int_1 anchorLink https://twitter.com/intent/tweet?url=https://twitter.com/Greenpeace/status/14007844025
06870786&text=%23LetsGreenOurCities
Text paragraph before the link:  Tag your mayor
Text paragraph after the link:  Use the hashtag #LetsGreenOurCities on Twitter @tagging your mayor to demand
a greener city
--------------
cc_gp_int_1 anchorLink https://www.instagram.com/greenpeace/
Text paragraph before the link:  Spread the word
Text paragraph after the link:  Use the hashtag #LetsGreenOurCitieson Instagram stories/posts to tell us why
you do it and why is it important to have green spaces in our cities
--------------
cc_gp_int_1 anchorLink https://es.greenpeace.org/es/wp-content/uploads/sites/3/2021/05/Greening-the-City_Gree
npeace.pdf
Text paragraph before the link:  Read the report
Text paragraph after the link:  Cities should be designed and planned, taking into account the benefits of na
ture. Mayors, urban planners and public officials must share this same goal.
--------------
cc_gp_int_3 anchorLink https://www.greenpeace.org/international/act/curso-internacional-de-liderazgo-en-el-vo
luntariado/
Text paragraph before the link:  ¿Prefieres unirte en español?
Text paragraph after the link:  Who can take part?
--------------
cc_gp_int_3 anchorLink /international/act/volunteer-leadership-training/#form
Text paragraph before the link:  Registration for the April 2020 training has closed. To be informed about th
e next opportunity to join please provide us with your contact details using the form above.
Text paragraph after the link:  Questions?
--------------
cc_gp_int_4 iframe - youtube video https://www.youtube.com/embed/videoseries?list=PLClXnL5aHwxXDRjfBIK8lpohmb
09dXwJF
Text paragraph before the link:  Watch and share these eye-opening films that explain how big oil and agricul
ture firms are deceiving us through offsetting scams
Text paragraph after the link:  Offsets distort land and livelihoods
--------------
```

Figure 8: Anchor links and iframes and corresponding contextual texts for documents containing the keyphrase *climate change* in the Greenpeace International corpus between the years 2019 and 2020.

Author Index